A century of Promises

Edited by
David Roberts

From an original manuscript by Rhona Ray with additional material gathered by June Shakeshaft.

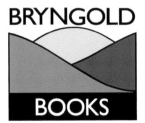

www.bryngoldbooks.com

First published in Great Britain in 2011
by Bryngold Books Ltd.,
100 Brynau Wood, Cimla,
Neath, South Wales SA11 3YQ.

www.bryngoldbooks.com

Typesetting, layout,
editing and design
by Bryngold Books

ISBN 978-1-905900-22-0

Printed and bound
in Wales by
Gomer Press,
Llandysul, Ceredigion.

Girlguiding in West Glamorgan
1912 — 2012

Byddwch Yn Barod

Be Prepared

Contents

About this book

This book owes its origins largely to the dedicated work of the late Rhona Ray, whose intention had been to produce a definitive record of West Glamorgan Guiding, in recognition of the movement's UK centenary in 2010.

During her lengthy involvement in Girlguiding, latterly as West Glamorgan Archivist, Rhona had amassed a sizeable body of information, chronicling the development of local Guiding.

Sadly, Rhona's declining health meant that the project was not realised in her lifetime, but it was decided to publish the book, using her writings as its foundation, enhanced by the inclusion of many additional contributions.

We are grateful to David Roberts for his efforts in editing the material, and, in a sense, drawing together the strands. The content within the pages, particularly the photographs, would certainly have exceeded Rhona's imagination. The collection of images depicts almost every aspect of Girlguiding through the years.

The pictures of the centenary celebrations in 2010 show the friendship and fun still gained by members of all ages, who have made the Promise, and with the approach, in 2012, of our county centenary, a double milestone is marked by *A century of Promises*.

I feel sure that Rhona would be pleased with the result of our efforts, and hope that everyone who reads this book will be rewarded with a fascinating trip down memory lane.

**June Shakeshaft, Archivist,
Girlguiding West Glamorgan**

Message of goodwill

The Promise may have changed over the century, but Guiding in West Glamorgan remains as strong and firm as ever.

I hope that everyone reading the written history of Girlguiding West Glamorgan, and looking at the many photographs in this book, will be reminded of the fun and friendship experienced in Guiding through the years.

There are excellent leaders and trainers in the county, and I know that Guiding in West Glamorgan will continue to flourish into the next century. Congratulations on the publication of A century of Promises.

**Felicity Ladbrooke,
Chief Commissioner for Wales**

Foreword

Many congratulations to all members, past and present of Girlguiding West Glamorgan on all that your county has achieved in the past 100 years.

This book celebrates the long and proud history of Guiding in the county. There will be many women and girls who will enjoy looking back through the words and pictures in A century of Promises with great fondness and be able to say 'I was there'.

Today, the Guiding story carries on, and we are as strong and relevant as ever in the modern world. Girls and young women continue to benefit from, and enjoy, safe girl time with friends, having fun and adventure together.

My very best wishes to everyone involved in Girlguiding West Glamorgan for success in all your endeavours as the county enters its second century.

Gill Slocombe.

**Gill Slocombe,
Chief Guide**

Girlguiding
West Glamorgan
leads the way

From the past,

through the
present,

and into
the future...

Introduction

Girlguiding is all about working as a team, something admirably reflected in the work that has resulted in the publication of this excellent record of the history of the movement in West Glamorgan.

Everyone involved deserves a big thank you for the part they have played, however great or small. While we commend Rhona Ray for her gatherings, she in turn was appreciative of the early efforts of Gwyneth Evans of Swansea Division for her foresight in recording facts about the first 50 years of Guiding in the city, along with the support of Joan Tainsh and Doreen Evans.

Rhona wanted the book to appear as a salute to how 100 years of Girlguiding UK had manifested itself in the county. Little did she realise that her efforts would contribute to something of a double achievement, for now the book has been developed into one which also closely focuses on a century of Girlguiding in West Glamorgan, coming as it does during 2011, the year that separates the two major milestones.

Sadly, Rhona didn't live to see the fruits of her labours, but she would surely agree that they have grown into a book which proudly stands as the starting post for celebrations to mark our county's centenary. Much more gathering of pictures and material has helped bring the book right up to date, mainly due to the magnificent efforts of our current County Archivist, June Shakeshaft. She has done a wonderful job. The result is a magical miscellany that now reflects every decade of our existence.

A century of Promises leads us through the early years where careful steps, taken by some very forward-thinking women, ensured matters were tackled correctly. It looks at how Girlguiding in West Glamorgan developed and spread down the years, resulting in the organisation that we can claim as our own today. Every aspect of Guiding is covered: Rainbows, Brownies, Guides, Senior Section and Trefoil Guilds along with the

activities they have successfully tackled and the challenges they have encountered down the years.

A century of Promises is interspersed with two colour sections, one showing how we celebrated the centenary of Girlguiding UK, the other portraying most of the units that comprise our county today, spanning its divisions and their districts. Between these is a wonderful selection of words and pictures that reveal many days in the life of Girlguiding in West Glamorgan. Parades and rallies, camping and travel, celebrations and adventures, all feature alongside moments that many individual members will treasure. These range from the making of a first Promise right up to the attainment of a Baden-Powell or Queen's Guide award.

It is interesting to see how our movement has evolved down the past 100 years, not only in the activities available to us, but also how we appear.

The book allows us to stand back and observe just how big a part we have played in the broader life of our community. Most importantly perhaps is the fact that we finally have an official and easily accessible record of our past.

For this, the support and guidance of David Roberts of Bryngold Books has been invaluable. His enthusiasm for seeing the project through and turning our dream into reality was unfailing.

A century of Promises is a salute to all those who have worked for the success of Guiding in West Glamorgan and in doing so ensured it has had a history to record. The book reflects the past 100 years and is one that will surely serve the county well during the next 100.

I hope you enjoy it!

**Mary Knill,
County Commissioner
Girlguiding West Glamorgan**

Dedication

This book is dedicated to the memory of the late Rhona Ray,
a stalwart of Girlguiding West Glamorgan and its long-time
archivist, without whose diligent efforts it would not have been
possible. Sadly, Rhona did not survive to see this book produced,
but we feel sure that she would have approved.

Sowing the seeds

1

Girlguiding, as anyone involved will know, began in 1909 when a group of determined young girls, dressed like their brothers in the Boy Scouts, gate-crashed a rally at Crystal Palace in London and demanded, by their very presence, that Scouting be adapted for girls. As a result, Lord Baden-Powell, the Chief Scout, promised to think about 'something for the girls', and in 1910 he persuaded his sister Agnes Baden-Powell to lead a new movement for them — the Girl Guide Association was born.

The 2nd Swansea (St James) Guides at Brooklands with their captain, Miss Victoria Talbot-Rice, 1918.

11

It wasn't long before the movement began to spread around the United Kingdom. By 1912 it had reached Swansea and the surrounding area. Here, under the leadership of Mrs J T Davies, a group of influential women met at her home, Kilgreen in Caswell Road, Mumbles, to form a committee whose aim was to establish a Girl Guide presence in the city and the neighbouring districts.

Likewise, under the guidance and leadership of Mrs Nora Gibbins, of Glynfelin, Neath Abbey, a similarly minded group met with the same aims for Neath and district.

With the seeds of the movement sown, the first Guide company was registered in June 1912 as the 1st Swansea (YWCA) Company. The captain was Miss Edith Bullock, one of the first warranted Guiders in Wales.

Miss Edith Bullock's Captain's Warrant, issued on October 8, 1912.

Guides march through central Swansea, 1914.

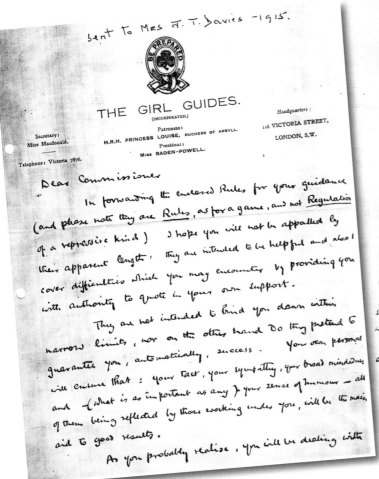

A letter written by Robert Baden-Powell to Mrs J T Davies, 1915.

Some of the early stalwarts of Girlguiding in West Glamorgan gathered together around 1922.

The first decade of Guiding in the county saw steady progress, so much so that by 1915 seven Guide companies had been formed, along with a single Brownie pack — the 1st Swansea (YWCA) Brownies.

In October 1915, the first meeting of the official Glamorgan Girl Guide Committee was held. It was chaired by Mrs J T Davies who had by then become a commissioner for Swansea. It is quite likely that she would have read to the committee a letter that she had recently received from Lord Baden-Powell. This letter

accompanied a set of rules that he stressed were intended to be used as rules of a game and not regulations of a repressive kind. Lord Baden-Powell also took the opportunity to highlight the importance of having a sense of humour.

Although Mrs Davies was addressed as a commissioner, the first recorded warranted commissioner for Swansea was Miss Victoria Talbot-Rice, who was appointed in 1918. It was, however, Mrs J T Davies who had steered the movement in the area

Early Glamorgan Girl Guides practise the art of semaphore signalling.

A group including Victoria Talbot-Rice, Olive Nichol and Miss Colman, 1919.

through uncharted waters, a journey that had culminated in that historic meeting at the YWCA in October 1915. This was to be the first of many more that would take place over the next 100 years, each one aiming to take Guiding in West Glamorgan ever onward.

Alongside these hard working committee members, the efforts of the many others whose dedication to the movement in West Glamorgan enabled Guiding to

move forward with such success during the last century must not be forgotten.

Many important decisions were taken at that first meeting in 1915. Among these was that committee members would meet four times a year on a Tuesday at 6pm; and that no badges would be awarded until a Board of Commissioners was formed.

Arrangements were put in hand for a general display and inspection of Guides by a Miss Helen Malcolm, a Guide commissioner from outside the area. This took place at 5.30pm on

Growth in Glam

Guides		Brownies	
1916	**1917**	**1916**	**1917**
474	681	17	145

Badges earned in 1916/1917

2nd Class 7	Needlework 1
Laundress 5	Artist 1
Cookery 2	

Saturday, November 6, 1915, at Oxford Street School, Swansea. This was a significant event because it meant that the Girl Guide movement in Glamorgan was now official.

In some parts of the county the Girl Guide Company was known as a club in the early days. One of the rules laid down by the 1st Mumbles Company, the second to be registered after the YWCA Company, was that 'Should a Guide be absent from club three times in succession, without sending an adequate written reason to the captain, her badge must be forfeited for a month, and she will become a dead Guide for that period. Then she will be given a second chance. If she is still absent, she will be required to resign from the Guide Company.'

Just as Guiding was really gaining a foothold in the county, Britain was plunged into the First World War. During this horrific conflict with Germany, which lasted from 1914 to 1918, it became apparent that Guides would prove invaluable to the war effort in many ways as they were able and willing to undertake a

Guides demonstrate first aid in Singleton Park, 1915.

multitude of tasks responsibly. These tasks ranged from Guides going once or twice a week to the YWCA hostel to help with the linen, to working in the kitchen or pantry at Parc Wern, later Parc Beck, in Sketty every Saturday morning for two or three hours.

The Red Cross also used Guides when they wanted messages and parcels delivered.

In fact a testimony was later given by the Red Cross about those Guides who had worked for them as being prompt, efficient and trustworthy.

Although it was wartime, local Guides still continued with their ordinary activities. They held a display at the end of June 1916 when badges were presented by Olive Nichol,

Guides demonstrate home nursing in Singleton Park, 1915.

The Chief Guide, Lady Olave Baden-Powell, during a visit to Swansea in 1919. This was her first visit to Guides in West Glamorgan.

17

A poster advertising a public meeting that was to be addressed by Lady Baden-Powell in 1919.

County Commissioner for Glamorgan. Other activities undertaken for the war effort included Mothers' Help Day, when Guides gave up their Saturdays to assist in people's homes. They would tackle jobs including gardening, cleaning, needlework and taking babies for walks. The money raised by completing such tasks could be as much as £1 which would be donated to various war funds.

The Guides also collected eggs for local hospitals, along with magazines, books and cigarettes for the troops overseas. This must have been a very exciting time for them,

being able to help with the war effort, albeit in a small way. It is interesting to note that some 8,972 badges were earned for war service by Guides nationally during 1917 alone.

That same year there were 12 Guide companies in Swansea, plus a number of others that by now had sprung up in various parts of the county such as Neath. In April 1917, the first County Executive Committee was formed from the Girl Guide Local Associations. Annual church parades also became a regular feature of Guiding at this time, alternating between various churches

A Guide rally in Singleton Park, Swansea, 1915.

and chapels that had links with companies. In 1919 Guides lined the route for visits to Swansea by the Prince of Wales and the Chief Guide, Lady Baden-Powell, who was on her first official visit to the county. During her stay she inspected the Guides at the Guildhall.

Around this time a special, well-attended training week was held at Ffynone by kind permission of Lady Mond. By the end of 1919, there were no fewer than 413 Guides and 108 Brownies in the Swansea Division. However, there were many more throughout the remainder of Glamorgan.

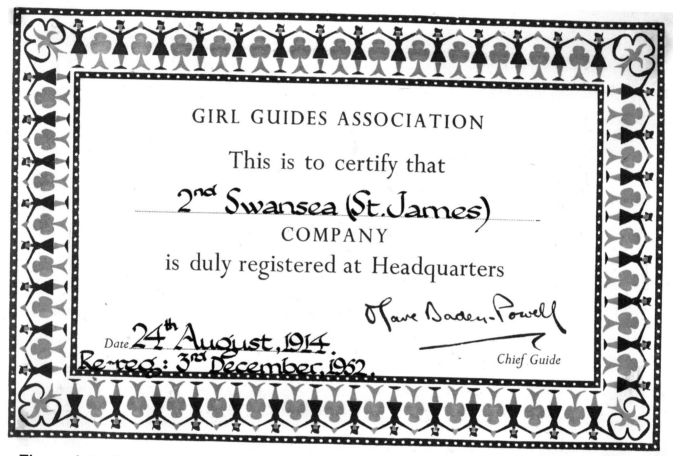

The registration certificate of the 2nd Swansea (St James) Guide Company. First listed in August 1914, they were re-registered in December 1952.

Members of an early Swansea Guide Company.

Roaring into the Twenties 2

By the arrival of the 1920s the enthusiasm of Guides and Guiders was greater than ever with the movement progressing in all directions. Such was its success that it became necessary to split the larger divisions in the county into districts, each with its own commissioner and a small executive committee, something which ensured better overall communication. In 1920 Swansea alone boasted 22 Guide companies, one Ranger company and 13 Brownie packs – a total of 793 girls. That year Princess Mary, later the Princess Royal, who was President of the Girl Guides, visited the city with her parents King George V and Queen Mary.

Brownies having fun playing games at Brynfield House, Newton, Swansea, 1922.

During their official visit to Swansea, Queen Mary was overheard to say to her daughter, the princess: "Look, Mary, there are some of your Guide friends."

Princess Mary inspected the Guides and spoke to several of them. She also shook hands with every Guider. Many Guides from Neath and Skewen were also present at this event.

During the inspection the 11th Swansea Guide Company won the division flag, competed for by all the Guides in that division. They received the flag from Princess Mary during a rally held at Sketty Hall.

In 1921 a camp site was acquired at Penrice on the Gower Peninsula through the kindness of Lady Blythswood, who lived at Penrice Castle. Lady Blythswood was County

The royal party meet the Guides during a 1920 visit to Swansea.

ROYAL NUMBER OF THE SWANSEA DIVISIONAL GAZETTE.

76, Walter Road,
Swansea.

August, 1920.

My dear Guiders,

What a lovely time we had during the Royal Visit. I don't think that we have ever had such a happy week end before, and when I think over it all again, I know that the proudest moment for the Swansea Guides was when we heard the Queen say to Princess Mary as she came towards us at Singleton, "Look, Mary, there are your friends again". It gave us all a thrill of pleasure to be called the Princess's "friends", and we realised more than we have ever done before that a true Guide is always a Friend to all. We have pledged ourselves to serve our King and Country, and when love and friendship are added to our promise how much easier it is to get into the true spirit of service. I also want to tell you that the happy time we all enjoyed so much during the Royal Visit was really due to each of you. You and your Companies were so splendid, and did such credit to the Division that everyone felt proud of each other. Miss Nicholl praised you very much, and was more than pleased to be one of the Swansea Division at the Inspection. Now it is up to each one of us to work and to be worthy of the praise that has been showered upon us, and I know you will do your best.

I remain,

Yours sincerely,

ELSIE M. ROCKE.

Miss Elsie Rocke's letter to Swansea Guiders after the success of the 1920 royal visit.

Tea time for a group of Guides on a camping visit to Penrice, 1922.

Members of an early Guide company with their captain, Miss E M Leonard.

1st Mumbles Brownies proudly showing off their uniforms in the 1920s.

Commissioner for the whole of Glamorgan at the time. The Guides were also allowed to use the loft over the stables at Penrice to store their camping equipment.

The expansion of the fledgling movement necessitated the formation of new divisions in the county, and in addition to Swansea, there were now divisions for Gower, Swansea Valley, Neath, and Afan Valley.

An arrangement was made with the YWCA at this time to use their premises at Eaton Crescent, Uplands, Swansea as a Guide Headquarters on two evenings a week and Saturday mornings at a cost of £20 a year.

A lending library of Brownie books was started with a grant of £5 from division funds. There was a borrowing charge of 2d per book. Local Associations were also being formed in this decade. The first, in Neath, began in September 1922 and was registered in January of the following year.

In 1922 members of the Guiding movement in the county collected two pounds, nine shillings and sixpence towards a wedding present for Princess Mary.

A magazine with the title of Guide Gazette was started about this time. Produced at six-monthly intervals, it contained lots of information and pictures. Though it was quite popular it only lasted for six years.

The Chief Guide, Lady Olave Baden-Powell, visited the county on June 5, 1924. The rally that had been arranged should have taken place at Singleton Park, Swansea, but the venue was changed to the Drill Hall where Lady Baden-Powell inspected more than 1,000 Guides from Swansea, Gower, Swansea Valley, Neath and Afan Valley.

In August 1924, Guides helped with tea and a pageant in the grounds of Penrice Castle. A Guide chair was competed for at the National Eisteddfod of Wales that year.

The 12th Swansea (Wesley) Brownies pose for a photographer during an outdoor activity.

Following this Mumbles Brownies and Guides decided to hold their own eisteddfod, complete with bards and a Gorsedd circle.

The summer of 1924 was a busy time for Guiding in the county. There were Guide camps and Brownie rallies – the first prize winners at one held on June 28, 1924, were the members of the 12th Swansea (Wesley) Pack.

In 1925 Mrs J T Davies, one of the founders of Guiding in the county, was elected Divisional Commissioner for Swansea, as well as remaining chairman of the executive

committee she had established in 1912. The committee was the forerunner of what later became known as the County Executive and meetings were run along similar lines to those of today.

At one such meeting, held in Cardiff on March 10, 1922, Lady Blythswood introduced herself for the first time as County Commissioner for the whole of Glamorgan. This situation remained for the following 25 years, until numbers became so large that the county was divided into Cardiff and East Glamorgan,

Swansea Guides at camp, 1928.

Morriston Guides resplendent in their uniforms, mid-1920s.

Central Glamorgan, and West Glamorgan. Even in 1922, fundraising was on the agenda. It appeared that, because of a change of administration, the vice-presidents' subscriptions had not been collected. The meeting was asked to consider inviting every district to make a donation, though it appears that no decision was reached on this.

Another means of raising money suggested was the hiring of a Guide film – no decision was reached on this either.

Two appointments were announced at this 1922 meeting – that of Mrs Gilbertson as Divisional Commissioner for the Swansea Valley, and Miss Rocke as Divisional Commissioner for Swansea.

It was confirmed at the meeting that the county standard would have three red chevrons on a gold background.

The next meeting was held in Swansea on August 16, 1922, when several more appointments were made, among them

that of the County President, the Countess of Plymouth. Finances, or rather the lack of them, reared their ugly head again at the November meeting in 1922. A minute of the proceedings states: The treasurer reported no money in the bank. Commissioners were reminded to send in their annual subscriptions of ten shillings (50p) from each district.

County meetings at this time were attended by district and divisional commissioners and chaired by the County Commissioner, Lady Blythswood.

The annual general meeting of 1925 was held on May 21 at Margam Castle, Port Talbot, the home of Lady Blythswood's sister-in-law, Mrs Andrew Fletcher.

In 1927 a new County Secretary, Miss Hodgens, was appointed. She had responsibility for arranging a visit to the county on August 11, 1928, by the Chief Scout and Chief Guide, who attended a rally at Margam Park.

A letter was subsequently received by the County Commissioner from Lady Baden-Powell expressing her pleasure at seeing so many Guides. The Guides were invited to take tea at the castle and were asked to provide an hour's entertainment for the guests.

Right: Girl Guides from Bryncoch during a ramble on the mountainside at Drummau, Skewen, 1928.

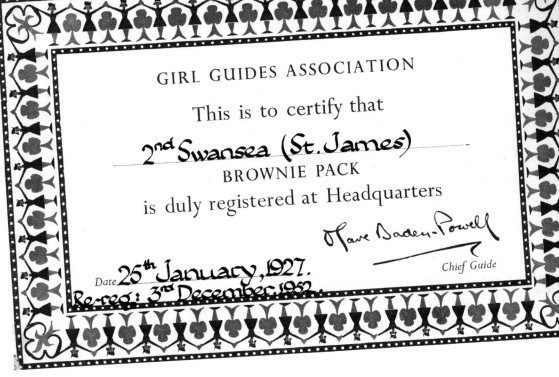

GIRL GUIDES ASSOCIATION

This is to certify that

2nd Swansea (St. James)

BROWNIE PACK

is duly registered at Headquarters

Olave Baden-Powell

Chief Guide

Date 25th January, 1927.
Re-reg: 3rd December, 1952.

The registration certificate of the 2nd Swansea (St James) Brownie Pack, January 1927.

29

In the latter half of the 1920s there was an increasing demand for Post Guide units for children with special needs, but more leaders were required to provide these. This was a clear demonstration that the Guide movement was already leading the field in integrating able-bodied and disabled Guides. This, of course, is a policy that has been developed and widely encouraged today.

Money was being raised by the county for Imperial HQ Buildings in London. Companies were asked to raise £1 each to provide a room at HQ at a cost of £500. Lady Blythswood represented both Wales and Scotland on the Building Fund Committee.

The decade ended on a sad note with the death, in 1929, of Lady Blythswood's husband.

The initial 2nd Swansea (St James) Brownie Pack, 1927.

Helping out in the Thirties 3

As the 1930s dawned, the Guide movement prepared to celebrate its coming of age – a 21 year milestone in those days. A range of festivities was originally planned for 1931, but the country's worsening economic and social conditions led to these being postponed until the following year. The Depression and the mass unemployment it brought, had a terrible effect on Britain with South Wales being particularly badly hit.

Going to camp might be fun, but there were still chores to be done, though that didn't appear to bother this happy group of girls at a 1930s Gower camp.

The 1932 county competition took the form of an eisteddfod, with the winners of divisional events proceeding to county finals.

There were over 800 entries. The final placings out of 12 for the area were:

3rd   Clydach

5th   Sketty

6th   Aberavon

9th   Neath

There were celebrations throughout the county during the year as the movement belatedly marked its anniversary.

Brownies, Guides and Rangers took part in many activities. Special Good Turns were completed. A Guide Sunday was held on May 29, with special services being organised throughout Glamorgan, while arrangements were made for Post Guides to wear their Trefoil badges throughout the week.

Other events included a holiday for 18 Post Guides at Penrice in June, with the girls in the care of Miss Marks and Miss Maureen Blair.

A Guide choir of 800 voices was formed nationally, of which a remarkable 390 were from Glamorgan. Wales was indeed the Land of Song!

Division Eisteddfod 1932.

Music.   Solo Singing.   'The Lover Task' arranged by Cecil Sharp
---------   Choir of not more than 10 voices. 'Tree Song'.
          Piano Solo.   Minuet in F. Mozart.

Recitation.
-----------   ' The West Wind' by John Masefield.

Art.   Design for a Patrol Log book cover, size 9 by 7 ins.
---   Lettering. The First Guide Law.
          Pictorial Chartt.for scoring points on a Patrol
                                          Competition.

Needlework.
----------- A pair of navy knickers to wear with Guide uniform.
          Embroidered cloth. Size about 10 by 16 ins.

Knitting and Crichet.

             A pair of socks. Foot not less than 6 ins.
             A Brownie cap.
             A piece of knitted or crochet lace, not less than ½yd.

Cooking. Six Welsh cakes.
----------   A 1lb pot of dried apricot jam.
             Sweetmaking.

Basket. Any article in raffia.
---------   Any article in cane.

Toymaking. Any toy.

Laundry. 2 white and 2 coloured hankies.

Literature.A Christmas story.
-----------   A poem on a hike.

Nature exhibit. Company entry.

          Plaster cast of footprint of 4 different animals or
          birds- drawing of each with noteson colour, food and
          habits.

Part of the programme for the 1932 county eisteddfod.

Camping, 1934-style for these adventurous Swansea Guides.

The Princess Royal at a Girl Guide rally in Singleton Park during her visit to Swansea, 1938.

A county standard was designed by Mrs Selby at this time and a camp for 55 Guides was held at Margam Park.

Due to the distress of many thousands of people during the 1930s as a result of high levels of unemployment and poverty, the county made an appeal for books, food and clothes. These were distributed to the needy and were greatly appreciated.

On Saturday, May 4, 1934, messages in semaphore were signalled across Wales by First Class Guides and Rangers. The message was a greeting to the Chief Scout and Chief Guide in London. All of these messages arrived safely at the London HQ.

Glamorgan was responsible for signalling from Garth in Breconshire over the mountains to the tower of Brecon Cathedral, and then on to the next county. Each girl signalled a distance of 15 miles.

For King George V and Queen Mary's Jubilee year, every Brownie Six and Guide Patrol in the county was asked to contribute a silver threepenny piece, the money going to the Prince of Wales Jubilee Fund. The collection eventually raised £34.00.

Lady Blythswood, County Guide Commissioner for Glamorgan with a group of divisional commissioners at a celebration dinner in Cardiff to mark 21 years of Guiding.

Some of the delegates who attended an annual meeting of Welsh Guides at Llandrindod Wells, between March 28 and April 1, 1935.

Swansea Guides during a rally at St Helen's sports ground, Swansea, 1937.

Guides demonstrating their first aid skills for the Princess Royal at Singleton Park, 1932. Looking on are Lady Davies, Chief Commissioner for Guides in Wales and other Welsh commissioners.

An amusing, though at the time serious, request was made by Glamorgan Guides as to whether the national Guide Headquarters could produce a Guide hat for less than 1/6d (7½p). The reply was that there was no way that they could produce a hat for less than the current price of 1/11d (almost 10p)!

At a county meeting on January 23, 1935, Lady Blythswood announced that she was to make available another camp site at Penmaen on Gower. The first camp held there, a training week for Guiders, took place during Whitsun 1936.

The first County Recorder was appointed in 1936 to keep in touch with former Guides. The position was the forerunner of the Trefoil Guild, which was still seven years away.

The Coronation of King George VI and Queen Elizabeth in 1937 saw many celebrations throughout Glamorgan. A pageant was held in the grounds of Cardiff Castle depicting the history of the county, and a mediaeval fair was enacted by Swansea and Gower Divisions. The Chief Guide was one of many distinguished visitors present.

The new King and Queen visited the county in July 1937. The Queen, in particular, showed great interest in all the Brownies, Guides and Rangers lined up to welcome them. In Swansea, Divisional Commissioner Mrs J T Davies was called forward by the Queen and congratulated on the smart turnout.

This same year brought about the formation of the 2nd Neath Guide Company. With 26 members, it was attached to St Joseph's Roman Catholic Church. It had been 14 years since the first company was formed, but it was not long before the movement began to flourish in the division.

Suggestions of sums to be contributed towards the Chief Scout and Chief Guide's Silver Wedding make interesting reading.

The amounts were a halfpenny for Brownies, one penny for Guides and one shilling for warranted Guiders.

During the latter half of the 1930s, Guides from Glamorgan represented two-thirds of those camping in Wales.

A Guide company conquers an ascent of Arthur's Stone at Cefn Bryn, Gower, 1934.

A bell tent was the order of the day for these Guides on a 1934 camp in Gower.

Washing up time again!

The first Brownie Pack Holiday in the county with Eagle Owl, Miss Hockin, her young charges, a dog and baby too! The year was 1937 and they were pictured near South Farm.

A poster for a fete and rally in the grounds of Sketty Hall, July 1935.

Some 1930s Brownies.

By now Brownie holidays too were being proposed. These became very popular and were the forerunner of what later became known as pack holidays.

As 1939 progressed and the political situation across Europe worsened, camp visits and holidays were suspended indefinitely when war was declared, in September 1939.

Once again, as in the First World War, the Guides had an opportunity to put their excellent organising skills to good use.

Glam goes camping
In the years at the end of the 1930s the county reported that —

147 Camps had taken place

3,496 Guides had taken part

14 Ranger camps had been held

110 Guiders had camped

4 Camps had been held at Penmaen

16 Guides from the county had travelled abroad to destinations such as Switzerland, Lithuania and Hungary

At this time there were more than 90 companies in Glamorgan

Manselton Brownies provided a 'Royal Coach' for the Princess Royal when she took part in Brownie Revels during a visit to Singleton Park in May 1938.

Requests were received from the ARP (Air Raid Precautions) for car drivers to help evacuate hospitals in the event of war. Members of the movement agreed, and also assisted with assembling gas masks, carrying out clerical work and generally helping local authorities whose employees had been called up for war service.

The decade ended on a sad note for the county with the death of the founder of local Guiding, Mrs J T Davies. Earlier in the year she had received the Medal of Merit for her 31 years' service to the Guiding movement.

The avenue of colours that greeted the Princess Royal during a rally at Singleton Park, Swansea, May, 1938.

I remember
. . . Scouting for Boys revealed all the mysteries of the movement to me as a 1930s Guide — **Joan Tainsh, Trefoil Guild member, former Guider, Trainer and Adviser.**

Guides marching up Windsor Road, Neath, during the town's annual civic parade, 1939.

The 2nd Sketty Guides
at camp, 1933.

Roman Bridge, Blackpill,
Swansea, provided a welcome
resting place for these Guides
out on a hike in the mid-1930s.

Swimwear was the order
of the day for many of
these Bryncoch, Neath,
Guides at Penrice in the
summer of 1937.

Bryncoch, Neath, Guides take a break during a mountainside ramble, 1933.

Swansea St Mary's Guide Company, 1933.

The 2nd Sketty Guides off to camp in 1934 with Miss I Hodgens and Miss G Evans.

Off to see the world

4

In the year that marked the centenary of Girlguiding, some 2,000 international members joined 5,000 members of Girlguiding UK at a very special camp at Harewood House, North Yorkshire. Not surprisingly, included among them were representatives from West Glamorgan. Indeed, travel has featured prominently in the exploits of the county's members throughout the decades. As Girlguiding spread around the world, county Guides took advantage of the opportunities for travel that this brought with it.

These girls from the 1st Bryncoch Guides couldn't have gone further west in mainland Britain for their camp in 1974.

The butterfly farm and maze at Ross-on-Wye was a hit with 4th Killay Guides.

. . . as was Warwick Castle. It was all part of the Great Guide Getaway.

Neath Ranger Guides with their Captain Miss Freda Gibbins on the platform of Neath General railway station on June 24, 1939. With rucksacks at the ready, they were about to embark on a two week trip to Switzerland. Just a little over two months after their return Britain was at war with Germany. Even though it was June, the girls were wearing raincoats and gauntlets! Miss Gibbins later became District, Division and then County Commissioner.

Many have visited the four World Centres owned by the World Association of Girl Guides and Girl Scouts. This has allowed them the opportunity to ski in the Swiss Alps, share in the excitement of a Mexican fiesta, experience the wonders of India or, closer to home, take in the bright lights of London.

For those who haven't ventured as far, there have been visits to locations and events spread across the British Isles. Each will have provided the chance to engage with Guides from other counties and become immersed in an extensive range of activities.

Many West Glamorgan Guides will have happy memories of such visits, some of which will surely be revived by the images on these pages.

Aboard a ferry to the Isle of Wight, 2010.

A group of 1st Manselton Guides in a church in Finland, 2010.

Isle of Wight 2010.

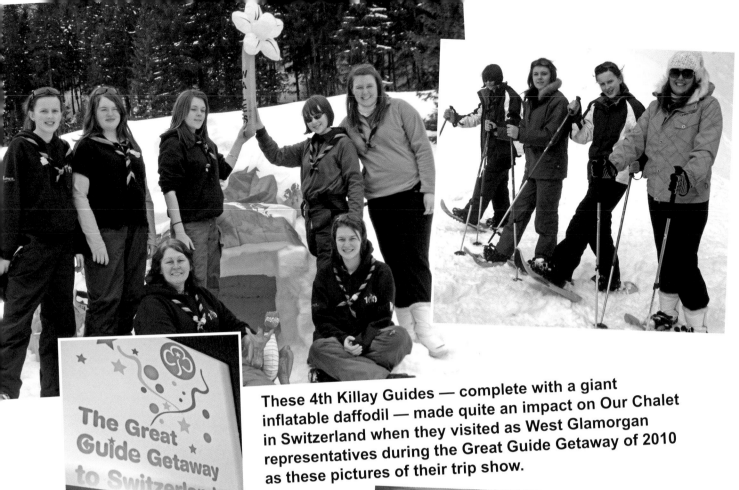

These 4th Killay Guides — complete with a giant inflatable daffodil — made quite an impact on Our Chalet in Switzerland when they visited as West Glamorgan representatives during the Great Guide Getaway of 2010 as these pictures of their trip show.

A group of 5th Sketty Guides in Hungary, 2005.

Members of No. 1 Swansea Air Ranger Flight, the only one in Wales, setting off for a fortnight in Austria from High Street station, Swansea, July 29, 1963, in the care of Lt M Gray and Miss E Webb.

This group of 30th Swansea Guides enjoyed a stay at Broneirion, 2001.

Rainbows have fun on a day out at Folly Farm as part of Rainbows Go Wild, 2010.

I remember

. . . going on a Guide centenary trip to Our Chalet in Switzerland. There were 650 girls, only five of them Welsh. I had so much fun and made lots of new friends
— Rhian Eaton, 1st Killay Guides

Have rucksack, will travel. 1st Baglan Guides leave for Switzerland, 1987.
They are wearing the UK neckerchief which is worn when travelling abroad.

Members of 4th Morriston Brownies on their pack holiday in America, 1996.

Sian Clwyd Roberts of 1st Cimla Guides at Alaska's Portage Glacier, in July 1995. Sian was chosen to represent British Guides as part of an experiment in international living, visiting Alaska for three weeks.

A group of 1st Aberavon Guides and Brownies outside Buckingham Palace during a trip to London on August 16, 1956.

A group of 1st Three Crosses Guides take a break during an arduous mountain walk in Switzerland when they visited Our Chalet, 2002.

A group of 2nd Clydach Guides take a break at Leeds Railway station on their way to the Great Guide Getaway Centenary Camp at Harewood House, Yorkshire, which took place from July 31– August 7, 2010.

A visit to Trafalgar Square, London.

Members of the 1st Baglan Guide Unit experience sunrise at the summit of Wildstrubel mountain, Switzerland, August 2000.

Centenary celebration 5

The West Glamorgan launch of the 100th anniversary celebrations of Girlguiding UK was an event that all those who were there will never forget. Under the watchful eye of County Commissioner Mary Knill, all sections of the movement in the county united to ensure that the occasion was a success. More than 1,500 participated in this colourful event which took place on September 6, 2009, approximately 100 years since a group of girls gate-crashed a Boy Scout Rally at Crystal Palace, London, determined that a similar organisation should be set up to provide for them.

Colour and spectacle were everywhere at the LC Swansea when West Glamorgan held a launch party to mark the start of county celebrations of the centenary of Girlguiding UK.

Members of Girlguiding West Glamorgan aged from five to 95 attended the launch which took place at the LC. To coincide with the event, an exhibition on the history of Girlguiding in the county was held at Swansea Civic Centre.

The Centenary year saw many events. Rainbows went wild at zoos and wildlife parks as well as holding Princess parties. Brownies took over castles and stately homes, while Guides got away to the Centenary Camp at Harewood House, Leeds and the four World centres, as well as many other destinations and events.

Throughout the year, members took part in The Greatest Adventure, a series of challenges based around the number 100, and many gained a special badge for completing this.

World Thinking Day on February 22, 2010, brought with it the theme of One World, One Beat. Members had the opportunity to take part in African drumming, line dancing, international singing, crafts, and many other activities.

Vision 2010 on October 20, saw every division link with units across the UK via the internet. At 20:10 20/10 2010 all the members renewed their promise before receiving a special Promise badge to be worn for a year.

As the colourful pictures here show, it was indeed a year to remember.

Scenes from the West Glamorgan launch party at LC Swansea on September 6, 2009.

More scenes from the centenary launch.

Some of the events which took place in West Glamorgan during the Centenary year of Girlguiding UK, 2010.

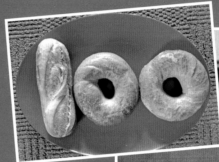

100 ways to salute a century

Some of the activities in which Girlguiding
West Glamorgan participated during 2010.

Neath

Glanymor

Afan Valley

County Camp Adviser and 2nd Port Talbot Guider Jenny Jones makes her Promise on a Dominican Republic beach. She did so at exactly the same time as her colleagues back home in the UK, 20:10 20/10 2010.

Gower and Glantawe

Something for the girls

6

When Baden-Powell announced that he would organise 'something for the girls', he could never have imagined that the modern day movement, in West Glamorgan as elsewhere, would be doing so much to maintain his ideals. Girls of all ages are presented with a multitude of opportunities to try their hand at new skills, involve themselves in challenging activities, and through global travel, broaden their horizons. The county is continually moving forward to ensure its members tackle the future confidently. Some of what they get up to certainly makes for a selection of interesting pictures.

There was time for some fun in the sun for these Guides who cooled off in a nearby stream during a visit to West Glamorgan Guide Activity Centre, Parkmill, June 2007.

Members of the 1st Three Crosses Guides who took part in the Lord Lieutenant's Service for Uniformed Youth Organisations, June 2010.

Brownies from the 4th Killay Pack prepare to play their part in a Uniformed Youth Organisations event.

New Programme handbooks being given out to Guides and Brownies in Castle Street, Swansea in 1968. The event was designed to raise awareness of the drive to bring Guiding up to date.

Members of the 1st Rhos Rainbows and Brownies during the presentation of a cheque to Margaret Pritchard of the British Heart Foundation. The money was raised by a sponsored skip.

Trefoil Guild
members give
a handbell
ringing recital
at Parkmill.

West Glamorgan Girl Guides
Netball Tournament
1989
Runners up.......

Three Crosses Winners.

Three Crosses, winners
of the West Glamorgan
Girl Guides netball
tournament in 1989.

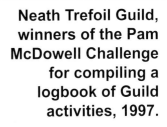

Neath Trefoil Guild,
winners of the Pam
McDowell Challenge
for compiling a
logbook of Guild
activities, 1997.

Three Crosses Guides,
Brownies and Rainbows
at Crwys Chapel, Three
Crosses on Armistice
Day, 2003.

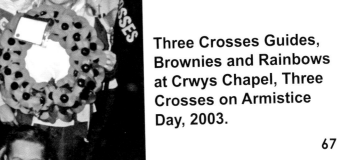

67

Girlguiding West Glamorgan Archivist, June Shakeshaft, surrounded by members of the Guiding family — a Rainbow, Brownie, Guide, Young Leader, Senior Section member and Guider, 2011.

Gathering wood for a camp fire at Parkmill, 2011.

Gower Crusaders, a special unit consisting of Guides and Rangers which was formed to assist other youth organisations in clearing the peninsula of litter and helping to make it more attractive to visitors, late 1960s.

Gower Crusaders gathering litter at Oxwich Bay during the late 1960s.

Brownies! They'll do anything to get in the picture.

The 3rd Port Talbot Guides packing boxes for Oxfam, 1962.

Leading the way for others to follow.

Members of Swansea Sea Rangers afloat at Fishguard, Whitsun 1950.

Cimla Guide Sarah-Louise Melbourne with her camp blanket of many badges.

Making friends at Llys Nini RSPCA animal rescue centre, Penllergaer.

I remember
... Having lots of fun as a Brownie and later Brownie Guider. It was great — **Mary Knill, County Commissioner.**

Adventure in the air.

71

Neath Scout & Guide Associations
Present the Show

CRYSTAL MANIA

by Prys Lewis
Directed by Kirstie Roberts
Musical Director Anthony Argyle

at the Gwyn Hall, Neath

April 2001
Thursday 12th,
Friday 13th
and Saturday 14th
at 7.00pm

Tickets
Adults £4.00
Children £3.00

SWANSEA GRAND THEATRE

MEET THE GANG 1973

THE SWANSEA SCOUT
AND GUIDE SHOW

PROGRAMME 10p

Swansea Grand Theatre
MEET THE GANG 1972
The Swansea Scout
& Guide Show

SWANSEA
GRAND
THEATRE
WITH
THE SWANSEA SCOUTS
AND GUIDES PRESENT

MEET THE GANG

1977
THE QUEENS SILVER JUBILEE

PROGRAMME 15p

SWANSEA GRAND THEATRE

MEET THE GANG 1978

Programme 15p

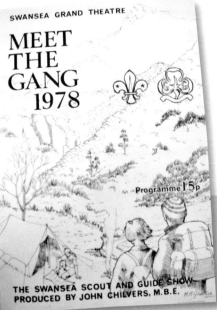

THE SWANSEA SCOUT AND GUIDE SHOW
PRODUCED BY JOHN CHILVERS, M.B.E.

Scenes from some
of West Glamorgan's
highly successful
Gang Shows.

A selection of programme
covers from successful
Gang Show productions.

Recipients of bronze swimming awards with County Commissioner Pamela Sutton at the 1997 annual general meeting of Girlguiding West Glamorgan.

Winners of the final swimming awards presented by the county, July 1995.

Sarah Davies, a member of the National Scout & Guide Orchestra, July 1997.

Fortitude in the Forties 7

The outbreak of war brought with it many restrictions. One such problem was that there were difficulties in finding halls in which the county's units could meet. One school-based company, the 23rd Swansea, was evacuated to Llandeilo, while many meetings had to be cancelled due to the black-out. Some camping was allowed, but this was governed by Home Office rules. Nevertheless, the Guide movement more than proved its worth in the county, as elsewhere, during the long years of war.

Guides with Princess Mary, the Princess Royal when she visited Swansea, 1949.

Guiding leaders at a civic function outside Swansea Guildhall, 1943.

Many garments of various kinds were knitted and distributed to Comfort funds, Mission to Seamen, Sailors' Society and others. Silver paper was collected, as were books and magazines for servicemen and women. Over £100 was collected by patrol leaders and sent towards the purchase of a Guide Air Ambulance and Lifeboat.

A Guides War Relief Fund was launched to help Guides and Brownies whose homes had been bombed. Swansea became a recipient of the fund after the devastating Three Nights' Blitz of February 19, 20 and 21,1941.

The Ministry of Food asked Guides and Rangers to organise emergency cooking in each street affected. It was decided to arrange for one cooker in every district to start with.

There was a memorial service held for the Chief Scout, Baden-Powell, who had recently died, at St Mary's Church in Swansea and across the county.

At a county meeting in Bridgend on December 13, 1941, Miss Freda Gibbins became Assistant County Commissioner responsible for Swansea Valley, Neath, Swansea and Gower.

Some of the former Christ Church Guides who attended a reunion of their unit,1946.

Port Talbot Guides
Ida Williams and
Lolita Antolin,
March 1941.

Members of SRS
Romola, the Swansea
Sea Rangers unit, 1947.

A Guide coffee morning
at Gabalfa, Sketty, 1947.

In 1942 camping resumed – provided that only small camps were held, that tents were camouflaged, that lighting regulations were strictly adhered to, and that suitable cover was arranged near the camp in the event of air raids. In total 250 Guides eventually camped in 1942, although Flemingdown Hut at the county camp site was damaged by enemy action.

The war effort continued thanks to the hard work of all members of the movement across the county. Help was given at the YWCA hostel, and Guides joined the WVS with their emergency feeding programme. A war service badge was awarded to three Guides from the 1st Mumbles Company, Swansea.

Hundreds more garments were knitted and distributed. A Salvage Campaign was supported, and more than 3,250 old and worn gramophone records were collected and money raised for various good causes.

In a resolution passed at a county commissioners' meeting, any pack or company raising money for charity had to keep some back for their own funds as they would not be asking the public for money for themselves again.

Swansea Sea Rangers, SRS
Romola Swansea, 1947.

Outside Swansea
Guildhall during a visit
by the Princess Royal
to the city, 1949.

On September 25, 1943, Lady Blythswood resigned as County Commissioner. Voting took place throughout the county as to whether it should be permanently divided into three counties, West Glamorgan, Central Glamorgan, plus Cardiff and East Glamorgan. The results were: 34 in favour, 22 against.
The result meant that the move for division of the county had been carried with a majority of 12 and the West Glamorgan Guide Association was born. With Miss Freda Gibbins as its first County Commissioner, the new Guide county covered the Afan Valley, the Swansea Valley, Neath, Swansea and Gower.

At the last committee meeting of the old Glamorgan area, an expression of appreciation for all Lady Blythswood had done for Guiding in Glamorgan was recorded.

Money was now being raised towards a B-P Memorial Fund to be invested by Guide Headquarters in War Savings Certificates. The idea was that at the end of the war this fund would then be devoted to the benefit of Guides everywhere.

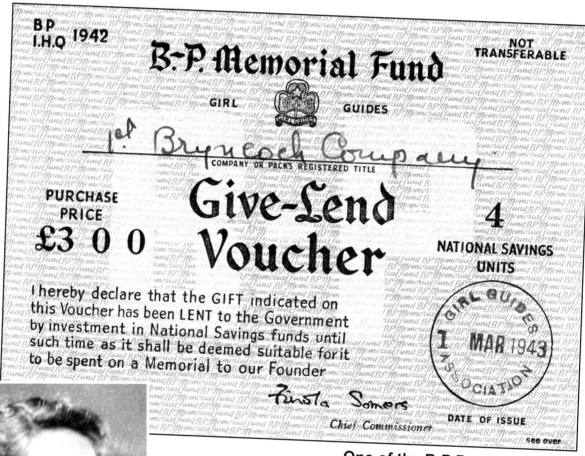

Ruby Nicholas who was the first member of 1st Manselton Company to become a Queen's Guide in 1947.

One of the B-P Bonds issued to raise funds for a memorial to the founder. This one, for £3, was issued to the 1st Bryncoch Company on March 1, 1943.

Chief Guide Lady Baden-Powell visited the county, and Lady Blythswood was invited to attend a meeting of Guiders and Commissioners at Swansea YMCA in order that a token of appreciation be presented to her on her resignation as County Commissioner. She received a silver ink stand with the following inscription:

'To our County Commissioner, Lady Blythswood, a token of affection from Commissioners and Guiders of Glamorgan 1922 -1943.'

After this, everyone was delighted to learn that Lady Blythswood had agreed to become President of the newly formed Guiding county of West Glamorgan.

With the formation of the new county it was decided to produce a newsletter twice a year. It was not entirely a new idea as a Guiders Gazette had been published in the 1920s.

By the time that the new Guide county of West Glamorgan was formed, Guiding was flourishing everywhere.

An empty shop was taken over by Local Association members to raise money for the movement. The venture raised £160, of which £150 was invested in Defence Bonds at three per cent. It had already been agreed that when packs or companies raised money a balance sheet should be submitted to division or district within a fortnight, keeping a percentage back for its own needs.

On February 10, 1944, Madam Maltowska, Chief Guide of Poland, paid a visit to West Glamorgan, addressed Patrol Leaders at one meeting and Commissioners and Guiders at a second.

When the war ended in 1945, West Glamorgan was well represented at the Victory Parade in London. By 1946 things were slowly, but thankfully, returning to normal.

Mount Pleasant and YWCA Guide Companies combined to pack comfort parcels for troops during World War Two, 1940.

Swansea Ranger Guides patiently queue for their lunchtime soup during a camp at Penmaen, Gower, 1949.

I remember

. . . Singing, playing games and making lots of things in Brownies. I loved every minute of it. I thought the uniform was great — I still have it — and enjoyed gaining all my badges. Such happy memories!
— **Jane Holmes, former 1st Glais Brownie.**

The 1st Parkmill and Penmaen Guide Company with Brownies outside the Gower Inn, Parkmill, joined by landlady, Mrs Morris, mid-1940s.

The big event of 1947 was the official opening of the Welsh Guide Headquarters at Broneirion in Llandinam, Mid Wales, by the Chief Guide. The event took place at Whitsun that year. Some Guide personnel stayed the weekend, with buses full of Guiders and Guides from the county going up for the day.

Money was collected in pennies towards a 21st birthday present for Princess Elizabeth. In addition she was also given a Guide brooch.

Throughout the county, divisional headquarters were being sought. At the time, Swansea had a room at the Red Cross HQ in Sketty Road.

In 1947 the first two Guides ever to be awarded their Queen's Guide Badge in Swansea, if not in the county, were Ruby Nicholas, of the 1st Manselton Company, and Sheila Smith, 1st Sketty Company.

A recruitment week was held in the county from February 22-29 when each Guider was asked to persuade one friend to join the movement in a similar role. Slides were made and shown on cinema screens urging people to come forward and help. This turned out to be a very successful appeal.

That same year, Rangers and Guides formed a guard of honour when the Princess Royal visited the county, while representatives of West Glamorgan attended the Wales Conference in Llandrindod Wells.

The highlight of the close of the 1940s was a visit to Cardiff and a nearby weekend camp attended by Princess Elizabeth in her Sea Ranger uniform. Eight girls plus a Guider represented West Glamorgan there: five Guides and three Sea Rangers.

Members of the 1st Bonymaen Guide Company, winners of the coveted Swansea Divisional Proficiency Trophy, late 1940s.

Sketty Brownies provide a guard of honour at a local wedding, possibly for their Brown Owl, 1949.

Flat out for the Fifties

The 1950s brought a huge increase in the number of Brownie and Guide units throughout the county. On May 1, 1950, a Message of Friendship from the Chief Commissioner of Guides in Britain was carried through the county, starting at Rhossili, Gower, by bicycle, lifeboat and the Mumbles Train. The message conveyed good wishes to a Belgian Guide delegate who was attending an international conference in Oxford. It was lodged with the Mayor of Swansea overnight for safekeeping before continuing on its way.

Sketty Guides hold a coffee morning at Brynawel, the home of Trevor Mort, 1955.

In November of the same year, Sea Rangers formed a guard of honour for Princess Margaret in London.

The only Sea Ranger Company in the county took part and was anxious to have its logbook signed by the Princess. This wasn't possible at the time, but it was suggested that if they sent it to Buckingham Palace it would be signed and returned. It was duly sent off and much to the delight of members was returned signed.

Another high point for the Sea Ranger unit was the launch by the Mayor of Swansea of their vessel SRS Romola, which went on to serve its members well for many years.

Two Rangers and nine Guides travelled to London for two days to take money, collected in pennies, by the county towards the cost of decorating Guide HQ. In addition, one tin of distemper from each district was also taken to assist with the project.

The 2nd Mumbles Brownie Pack, June 1951.

Members of SRS Romola, Swansea Sea Rangers, march smartly up Wind Street, during a Festival of Britain parade, 1951.

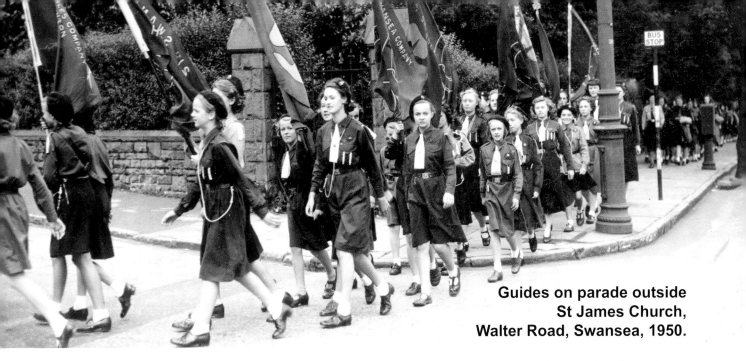

Guides on parade outside St James Church, Walter Road, Swansea, 1950.

The Festival of Britain was held in 1951 and on June 2, 550 Rangers and Guides marched through Swansea, many companies with their colours, as a celebration of this grand event.

Two overseas Guiders were entertained in Swansea, one from Luxembourg, one from the USA, and later in the year a party of Italian Guides arrived. They were given an official welcome by the Mayor.

A combined Scout and Guide rally was held at Singleton Park, attended by the Mayor and about 3,000 people, while eight Guides from the county attended a camp at Beaconsfield.

The Chief Guide visited the county in October, 1952, hosting two meetings, one for the Local Association and one for Rangers and Guides.

A Cadet Company was also started in order to provide Guide Leaders for the future. They were distinguished by a white band around their hats.

Coronation Year, 1953, was a very busy one for Guiding in the county. Several processions took place, plus a carnival procession with floats depicting Ranger, Guide and Brownie activities. A training weekend was also fitted in at Kilvrough Manor, Gower.

West Glamorgan Cadet, Jennifer Bentley-Jones who, along with seven other Guide movement representatives, took a record of its service tribute to Queen Elizabeth II at Buckingham Palace on the occasion of her Coronation, June 1953.

St James Brownies, 1954.

The 1st Manselton (St Michael's) Guide Company in Singleton Park, Swansea, with Captain Joan Tainsh and alongside her Audrey Baptist (later Mawson) 1950.

Cadle Brownie Pack, 1952.

Swansea Guides at a civic parade in St James Church, 1953.

Guides, Brownies and Cubs too, at St Paul's Church, Sketty, on their way to their annual church parade, 1958.

The Chief Guide's visit to Swansea, 1957, for the 5th All Wales Rover-Ranger conference, when she turned all the 'bigwigs' off the platform.

A Royal visit to the city by the Queen and Prince Philip offered another opportunity for Guides and Rangers to parade.

Later, eight Guides went to London to see an ice show at Wembley in aid of Guide funds. One was selected to form part of the guard of honour for Princess Margaret when she visited the spectacular event.

As the decade rolled on, trainings became a regular feature of the Guide calendar. County Guides were also starting to represent Wales at international camps. There was a further proud moment when the Sea Ranger crew of SRS Romola was granted Admiralty recognition, the first crew in Wales to be recognised in this way.

Rover-Ranger clubs were now opening so that older Scouts and Rangers could socialise.

St James Brownies visit camp, 1952.

Swansea Sea Rangers, early 1950s. The company met at St Helen's Junior School, every Friday. Skipper Elaine Sharpe is seen teaching them knotting.

Square dancing was a very popular activity in these clubs and drama productions often took place.

In 1956 the Chief Commissioner's Patrol Challenge was entered by companies all over the British Isles. The Heather Patrol, of the 1st Manselton Guide Company, was the first to complete the test in Great Britain.

Meanwhile Extension Guide companies were flourishing. This was Guiding for special needs girls. They were taken on holiday to Broneirion by a team of very dedicated helpers.

Camping was again in full swing, with many companies travelling overseas to various destinations including the Channel Islands. In one year alone 483 Cadets, Rangers and Guides headed off to camp. Brownies were now being taken on Pack Holidays, usually to Providence Guide Hall in Bishopston or Gorwelion in Mid Glamorgan.

The centenary of the birth of Baden-Powell was celebrated all over the country, and West Glamorgan played its full part. Many services were held at the same time as one at Westminster Abbey.

A team of dedicated helpers at High Street station, Swansea, accompanying two special needs Guides off on a holiday to Broneirion, 1956.

The 4th Swansea (St David's) Brownie Pack in a Corpus Christi parade near the Slip Bridge, Swansea, 1953.

Chief Guide Lady Baden-Powell, attending the Rover-Ranger Conference at the Brangwyn Hall, 1957.

Neath Rangers with their leaders during a civic parade through the town, late 1950s.

St James Brownies and Guides at a rally in Singleton Park, 1953.

The 2nd Swansea (St James) Guides, October 1953.

In May 1957 the county came second in the Welsh Eisteddfod at Llandinam, and first in the Senior Section. Busloads of Guides went to Llandinam to support their colleagues.

The county hosted Welsh conferences for Rovers and Rangers, and a nationwide one for Guiders.

The appointment of a County Trefoil Guild Recorder in the late 1950s saw a resurgence of interest in Trefoil Guilds, of which the most successful at the time was the Christ Church group. An Air Ranger Flight was also started, which was then the only one in Wales.

It was at this time that the national Salvation Army Life Guards were amalgamated with the Girl Guide Association. This move immediately swelled the number of active Guides in West Glamorgan to 1,600.

Money was being raised throughout the county in aid of world refugees and the annual parade of the Swansea Division in 1959 was rather special, as the last parade held at St Mary's had been nearly two decades earlier, shortly before the church was destroyed by bombs during the infamous Three Nights' wartime blitz of Swansea.

Sadly, at the end of the decade, County President, Lady Blythswood, died. She had been a pioneer of Guiding in Glamorgan and a great supporter, providing the county with camp sites at both Penrice and Penmaen.

The 2nd Swansea (St James) Guides, May 1959.

St James Brownies, 1952.

Three members of Swansea Air Ranger Flight alongside an aircraft at Swansea Airport, mid-1950s. At the time it was the only such unit in Wales.

1st Townhill Brownie Pack, 1954.

Members of Swansea Air Ranger Flight, mid-1950s.

St James Guides on parade, 1956.

Guide captain Ray Charles, centre,
with her 1st Neath Company, mid-1950s.

A majestic reward

Guiding has always provided its members with opportunities to achieve many different goals, badges and awards through hard work, determination and enterprise. The variety of badges available may have changed with the times, but girls in West Glamorgan have always enthusiastically embraced the concept of recognition for endeavour. The Queen's Guide Award is the highest that members of Girlguiding UK can aim for. Those who have attained it can feel justifiably proud of their achievement.

Five 1st Manselton (St Michael's) Guides with their captain Joan Tainsh, receive Queen's Guide Awards from County Commissioner Catherine Kwantes on December 22, 1962. They are Diana Vanstone, Carol Edwards, Elizabeth Collins, Elizabeth John and Gillian Beebee.

A presentation of a Queen's Guide certificate to Helen Jones of the 2nd Sketty Guide Company at Stewart Hall.

Queen's Guide June Rees, 1958.

The Queen's Guide award is based on the concepts of personal challenge and participation and is divided into five sections: service in Guiding; outdoor challenge; personal skill development; community action and residential experience where participants spend two nights and three days away from home with new people.

Although originally awarded to Guides, it is now only attainable by members of the Senior Section, including Young Leaders and Leaders, aged between 16 and 25. The syllabus must be completed within three years and before the member's 26th birthday. The emphasis in the current syllabus is on self challenge rather than a prescribed set of tasks. Since the scheme's creation 60 years ago it has been awarded to 20,000 young women. Some of the West Glamorgan recipients can be seen here. There are many more.

Divisional Commissioner for Swansea, Jean Morgan, presents a Queen's Guide award to Rosemary Kirby of the 2nd Swansea (St James) Guides, October 20, 1961.

Queen's Guides Ann Stone and Pamela Bastow, receive their awards, 1962.

Judith Morgan, who was the first Queen's Guide in the 2nd Sketty Company, receives her badge on October 2, 1959.

Queen's Guide Rosemary Kirby, 1961.

Jean Morgan presents a Queen's Guide award to Rosemary Bazzard of the 1st Morriston Guides, January 29, 1960.

Queen's Guides Fiona Williams, Ann Parker and Anne Lloyd of the 1st Bishopston Company proudly show their certificates to Guider Nora Peacock, late 1970s.

Valerie Toose, Jennifer Morgan and Alyson Davies, members of the 1st Waunarlwydd Guides, receive their Queen's Guide Awards, May 1973.

Laura Derrick of 3rd Port Talbot Guides receives her Queen's Guide badge and certificate from Mrs Olive Bray, Afan Valley Division Commissioner, 1981.

Hilda Davies of the 3rd Swansea Unitarian Guides receives her Queen's Guide Award from County Commissioner Jean Morgan, July 20, 1962.

County Commissioner Catherine Kwantes presents a Queen's Guide certificate to Mary Rogers of 2nd Sketty Guides, May 26, 1962.

Janet Taylor of 1st Crynant Guides with her Queen's Guide award, February, 1971.

Anne Richards of the 1st Blackpill Guides receives her Queen's Guide badge from Catherine Kwantes, July 1961.

Mrs Jean Morgan presents Queen's Guide Awards to Sheila Hall and Rosemary Stone of 1st Blackpill Guides, April 2, 1965.

A reunion of Queen's Guides, believed to be the first such reunion in the country, January 11, 1962.

Queen's Guide certificates for Gail Toogood, Elizabeth Hoare, Susan Baulch and Jean Lewis, members of 2nd Sketty Guides.

Cimla Guide Nia Hopkins receives her Queen's Guide Award from County Commissioner Carol Clewett, March 10, 1995.

Elizabeth Lewis and Janet Taylor receive their Queen's Guide awards from County Commissioner Jean Morgan, February 1971.

Queen's Guides Ira Davies, Carol Willis, Carole Morris and Katherine Jones, 1973.

Janet Molloy, the first member of the 1st Townhill Guide Company to become a Queen's Guide, receives her award from Divisional Commissioner Jean Morgan on March 12, 1965. Looking on are Swansea North District Commissioner Mrs H Davies and Miss M Ormerod, Guide Captain since the company was founded in 1938.

Swansea Divisional Commissioner Jean Morgan presents a Queen's Guide Award to Judith Stroud of the 1st Mumbles Company, at St Peter's Church Hall, Newton, 1965.

Queen's Guide Janet Morris, 1975.

Swansea Divisional Commissioner Jean Morgan presents the Queen's Guide Award to Charlotte Thompson of 2nd Sketty Guides, February 1966.

Queen's Guides Adela Mills-Davies and Judith Canning, 1966.

County Commissioner Carol Clewett presents Sian Clwyd Roberts of 1st Cimla Guides with her Queen's Guide certificate, September 1996.

Swinging in the Sixties 10

The 1960s was another significant decade for Girlguiding West Glamorgan. With its dawn came the Golden Jubilee of Guiding and a busy time all round. On Thinking Day a county service was held at St Mary's Church, Swansea, to celebrate this special milestone year. The church was full with Guiding personnel, and no fewer than 52 Colours were proudly paraded. County Guides again showed they cared in 1960 by raising £400 to help swell a fund set up to aid displaced persons in Refugee Year.

The first unfurling of a new county standard by Jean Morgan, Divisional Commissioner along with Gwyneth Evans, secretary; Judith Morgan, West Glamorgan Cadets and Ann Morgan, 2nd Sketty Guides, 1960.

During the summer of the same year a Guide and Scout rally was held at Singleton Park, Swansea, with the whole county participating. The Chief Guide, Lady Baden-Powell, arrived at the beginning and stayed throughout the afternoon, despite inclement weather. There was a fine march past, and the Brownies did a gallop. This special year saw many Guides and Guiders represent the county at Golden Jubilee celebrations in London while a party of Cadets visited Our Chalet in Switzerland. This is one of four World Centres established by the Guide movement, and is the first and oldest of them. The others are Pax Lodge in London, Our Cabana in Mexico and Sangam in India. Each centre is run by a small international team of professional staff along with volunteers.

Back at home, to help celebrate the year, Swansea Corporation arranged to have the floral clock at the Slip on the city foreshore set out in a pattern of Guide badges and emblems. The parks department of Neath Borough Council also planted a fine floral clock in the town's Victoria Gardens. To mark the Jubilee the County Executive

County Commissioner Catherine Kwantes with the Mayor and Mayoress of Swansea before the West Glamorgan AGM, 1960.

Members of the 1st Caereithin Guides at a party attended by Jean Morgan, Divisional Commissioner for Swansea, 1960.

A magnificent raised flower bed in Victoria Gardens, Neath, grown to salute 50 years of Guiding.

Judith Morgan, 22, a Guide Captain in Somerset but formerly a member of the 2nd Sketty Guides, and Susan Miles, 16, of 2nd Swansea Guides, who were chosen to represent Wales at an international Scout and Guide Jamboree in Iceland.

Chief Guide Lady Baden-Powell (fourth from left) arrives at Swansea's High Street station to attend the Golden Jubilee rally in Singleton Park, July 14, 1960. She was met by the County Commissioner for West Glamorgan, Catherine Kwantes.

The Brownie gallop at the Golden Jubilee rally in Singleton Park, Swansea, July 16, 1960.

Girls from the 2nd Killay Brownie Pack at the rally.

Guides lead the Commonwealth Youth Sunday parade in Princess Way, Swansea, May 14, 1961.

commissioned the making of a West Glamorgan standard depicting all aspects of the county's life. This was first seen at the rally in Singleton Park on July 16, 1960.

The standard was designed and made by Mrs E H Martin, head of the School of Embroidery at Swansea Art College.

The Jubilee celebrations had brought the movement to the attention of many more young people and the 1960s proved to be a time of clamouring to join the movement, so much so that in the county more and more

Brownie packs, Guide companies and Ranger units opened up. Trainings were being organised on a regular basis, both for new Guiders and the more experienced.
These covered all topics concerned with the correct running of units throughout the county. Attendance was in excess of 30 for every session. Although Extension Guide companies had been in operation since the 1950s, regular trainings were now given to those leaders too.

The Guide Association has always put a heavy emphasis on training its leaders, particularly

The dedication of a new county standard at St Mary's Church, Swansea, April 17, 1961. The standard was carried by Carol Davies, escorted by Judith Morgan and Joan Baulch of West Glamorgan Cadet Company.

These girls of the 2nd and 3rd Mumbles Brownie Packs had just presented 50 gifts to orphans of Dr Barnados. They are at the Guides loft, Newton, during a visit from Mumbles District Commissioner, Miss M Blair, December 1961.

Members of the 3rd Swansea Unitarian Guides collecting for the National Children's Home. They presented their collection boxes at the Festival of Queens at the Brangwyn Hall, 1961.

Guides often make the news as this cutting from the South Wales Evening Post in 1962 shows.

Duke's award for girl

JUDITH MORGAN, 18-year-old elder daughter of Mrs. Jean Morgan, Swansea Division Commissioner for Girl

those working with special needs children. It can be proud of its record on training, something that has always been supported in West Glamorgan, something which continues to this day.

Camping and Pack Holidays continued to be one of the most popular activities, with about 40 per cent of Guides camping, and 12 Brown Owls obtaining their Pack Holiday Permits.

The senior branch of the movement took on the challenge of the Duke of Edinburgh Award scheme. Cadet Judith Morgan and Air Ranger Anita Morris, were the first in the county to achieve the gold award and may well have been the first two in the Commonwealth, something which can be considered a great source of pride for the county.

Meanwhile, each of its divisions was working hard to raise money to build its own headquarters. Neath was the first to achieve this goal when its HQ was officially opened on June 1, 1964, by Lady Baden-Powell. This was followed four years later by Swansea Division in 1968. Their building was again opened by Lady Olave Baden-Powell. The Afan Valley headquarters was opened soon after in 1969.

A ticket for a 1962 event to raise funds for Swansea Headquarters.

SWANSEA SCOUT GUIDE H.Q. BUILDING FUND

Bring & Buy Coffee Morning

IN THE GARDEN OF
MYRTLE COTTAGE, HORTON
By kind permission of Mr. and Mrs Gordon Hayes
WEDNESDAY 16th JUNE 10.30.a.m. to12.30.a.m.
ADMISSION 2s6d
IF WET, AT HORTON VILLAGE HALL

Lady Olave Baden-Powell accompanied by Neath Divisional Commissioner Freda Gibbins at the official opening of Neath Divisional Headquarters June, 1964.

Having fun at camp.

Chief Guide Lady Olave Baden-Powell during the opening of the new Guide Headquarters at Bryn Road, Brynmill, Swansea.

THE SWANSEA SCOUT - GUIDE BUILDING FUND
(MUMBLES DISTRICT)

The House of Moriarty

have pleasure in presenting their

Autumn & Winter Millinery Collection

at the

DOLPHIN HOTEL, SWANSEA,

on

WEDNESDAY, SEPTEMBER 23rd, 1964

Coffee and Biscuits served from 10.15 a.m.   Hat Parade 11.0 a.m.

TICKET 5/- (inclusive).

A ticket for a fund raising fashion show, 1964.

Members of Swansea (St James) Guides on their way to camp in Ulster, August 1961.

County Commissioner Catherine Kwantes presents the Queen's Guide Award to Elizabeth Hunt of the 1st Mumbles Company, September 1962.

Thinking Day 1962.

West Glamorgan was always in the vanguard of any new ideas that were being tested so it came as no surprise when the first joint Guide and Scout camp within the county was held at Cadoxton, near Neath. Human nature took its course and a number of Guiders met their husbands-to-be at that camp!

Despite all the money needing to be raised at home for one cause or another, the county still managed to raise £400 to be used by the Save the Children organisation in Swaziland.

For several years during the 1960s a working party had been meeting in London and was drawing up a new programme for all sections of the movement, plus redesigning the Guide uniform in order to bring Guiding up to date and relevant to current members.

This took place in 1968, and in order to gain maximum publicity for the handbooks for the new programme, they were given out to Guides in public places and strategic points throughout the county.

A group of Guides during a visit to the original Scout and Guide Headquarters at Bryn Road, Brynmill, Swansea.

Inside St Mary's Church, Swansea, during the Brownie Jubilee service, May 8, 1964.

A new era in Guiding was about to begin, incorporating some old ideas, but including more up-to-date methods of enjoying Guiding. This was to take the movement into the 1970s and beyond.

The latter half of the decade saw many events in which local Guides and Brownies were involved. The National Eisteddfod of Wales was held in Swansea and Guiding was promoted on the Maes or eisteddfod field, with stalls and displays.

Gower Crusaders were formed during this time. The initiative saw Guides and Rangers form working parties to help clean up Gower for visitors. Along with other youth organisations, they helped by cleaning rubbish from beaches and manning a countryside caravan. 'Leave the countryside and seashore as you found it' was the motto.

The decade was rounded off by special celebrations for the Investiture of the Prince of Wales at Caernarfon and his subsequent

The oldest Guide Company in Swansea Division, the 2nd Swansea (St James) celebrated its Golden Jubilee in 1964. The event was marked by a social evening at St James Church Hall on May 29 of that year.

A congratulatory telegram from Swansea Division for St James Guides on their 50th anniversary in 1964.

Cwmavon Brownie Pack with their leaders, 1966.

Brownies line up before the Jubilee Service at Swansea's St James Church, May 1964.

Swansea Division
Girl Guides
SWIMMING GALA
18th Oct. 1966
Presented to 1st Blackpill Company
on being winners
of the Elizabeth Leonard award
Cup.

The 1st Blackpill Company were the 1966 Swansea Division swimming gala champions.

Guides demonstrate the bulldog spirit by helping with the distribution of leaflets to launch the Winston Churchill Memorial Fund, March 1965.

tour of Wales. When he visited West Glamorgan, Rangers, Guides and Brownies formed guards of honour along the way. Some Rangers were invited to Cardiff Castle to make Welsh cakes for the Prince.

Finally, Swansea received city status during the Investiture year of 1969, giving even more opportunities for the movement to show how well it could perform at ceremonial occasions.

THE SWANSEA GIRL GUIDES ASSOCIATION
SCOUT-GUIDE HEADQUARTERS BUILDING FUND

A Bring & Buy
Coffee Morning

To be opened by Mrs. J. T. MORGAN, J.P.

at THE STEWART HALL, SKETTY,

on WEDNESDAY, APRIL 28th 1965,
10.30 — 12.30

Stalls - Competitions - "Nearly New" Clothes Shop

TICKETS 2/-

More fund raising events from 1965.

This group of Rangers was tasked with making Welsh cakes for Prince Charles when he paid a visit to the county.

Lady Baden-Powell during a visit to officially open the new Neath Divisional Guide Headquarters, June 1, 1964.

I remember
. . . doing work for my badges. I felt really proud, a sense of achievement that I had done something on my own.
— **Angela Morris, former Glanymor Brownie.**

Mrs Sidney Heath, second from left, being presented with a Guide publication by Brownies Joanna Buse and Beverley Jones after opening a garden party in aid of the Scout and Guide HQ Fund. Looking on are Jean Morgan, Divisional Commissioner, and Mrs M C Edwards-Jones, at whose home in Gower Road, Sketty, the event took place in June, 1965.

Saluting the Seventies 11

By the advent of the 1970s Girlguiding in West Glamorgan was thriving. Interest in the movement across the county was at an all time high and more girls than ever before were involved, in all a total of 4,926. There was plenty to keep them occupied. After an absence of 44 years gang shows returned, county Guides helped make an LP record and Ranger Guides celebrated their Diamond Jubilee. In 1977 the county was also involved in events to salute the Silver Jubilee of Queen Elizabeth II.

Guides, guests and officials witness the cutting of the ribbon that signalled the opening of the hut at Penrice Camp Site, June, 1974.

As part of plans to celebrate the Diamond Jubilee of the Girl Guide Association, an All Wales Diamond Jubilee Eisteddfod was held at Gregynog, near Newtown. Princess Margaret visited the event and a poem submitted by a West Glamorgan Ranger Guide won in its section.

Also as part of the celebrations a party of 20 Guides from the county attended a Thanksgiving service at Westminster Abbey and Westminster Cathedral on May 16, 1970.

During the summer a Guide and Scout rally was held in Singleton Park, attended by Mrs Ann Parker-Bowles, Chief Commissioner of the Commonwealth.

Training camps and international visits were high on the county programme at this time.

Following a successful LP record of Brownies, Guides, Rangers and Guiders called Singing Along with the Girl Guides, produced by the BBC, the movement was asked whether another could be made, with the suggestion of basing it around a competition.

Amazingly, a quarter of a million members of the movement took part through heats at county, regional, and finally at United Kingdom level. Morriston and West Glamorgan Rangers, together with Neath Rangers won places to sing on the new LP along with other finalists from Guiding's National Festival of Song.

Cadoxton, Neath, Brownies during a presentation ceremony, 1973.

I remember
. . . when I was a Guide in the 1970s sitting around campfires in the dusk and singing, with camp blankets wrapped around us to keep us warm, while toasting marshmallows; polishing badges for an inspection, gang shows, challenges, fun and friendships.
— **Lesley Mathews, Deputy Chief Commissioner, Girlguiding Cymru.**

West Glamorgan
Girl Guide Association
This is to Certify that
1st NEATH RANGERS
gained FIRST PLACE
in the
COUNTY JUBILEE EISTEDDFOD
MARCH, 1970   Jean Morgan

A rally for the
Diamond Jubilee
of the Guide
movement, 1970.

Townhill Guides on
parade at St Nicholas
Church, 1973.

Princess Margaret, President of the Guide Association, talks to West Glamorgan County Commissioner Jean Morgan during the All Wales Eisteddfod at Gregynog to celebrate the Diamond Jubilee of Guiding, 1970.

Members of the 5th Neath Brownie Pack present a cheque to aid the children's ward at Neath General Hospital, Penrhiwtyn, Neath, 1974.

In 1971 the first Scout and Guide Gang Show for 44 years was held at the Grand Theatre, Swansea.

It came about through the enthusiasm of John Chilvers, the Grand's long serving administrator. The theatre was being redecorated at the time and the person in charge of the electrical work was wearing a Scout badge. Mr Chilvers saw it and asked why there was no Gang Show in Swansea.

Within a short time of that chance encounter plans were put in hand to hold one. About 150 Cubs, Brownies, Scouts, Guides and Rangers took part. The production, entitled Meet the Gang, was so successful that it was repeated every year until 1981.

Meanwhile, Good Turns continued to feature prominently among the activities of the county. Typical of these was when the 2nd Skewen Guides and Brownies raised money to

help buy a guide dog for a blind person. The county also 'adopted' foreign children afflicted with leprosy and raised money for eye clinics in Third World countries.

Closer to home Extension Guide and Extension Ranger units were active. Although small in number, they managed to follow as far as possible the Guide programme. One of their achievements was making knitted squares that were made into blankets which were presented to elderly people in the county.

More Guides than ever were camping, further afield as well as locally, and many Guide units were being taken abroad to camp by their adventurous Guiders.

A successful Scout and Guide conference was held at Swansea University in 1971, a year in which the county was represented at many international events, while visits to the county were made by overseas Guides. Pack Holidays

Duke of Edinburgh Gold Award winners from Wales, including some from West Glamorgan, at Buckingham Palace, 1970.

were proving to be very popular with the younger section of the movement and more and more Brownie Guiders gained their Pack Holiday Permits to facilitate this.

By 1973 members in the movement in the county had reached an all-time high of 4,926. This number was achieved due to the fact that more people were coming forward as leaders and new units were opened in outlying areas, particularly in Gower and the Swansea Valley divisions.

The number of Guides and Rangers working towards the Duke of Edinburgh Award also increased considerably, with the resulting successful gold awards being presented at Buckingham Palace in London by Prince Philip.

The 22nd World Guide Conference was held in Sussex University in July 1974. It was the first to be held in the UK for 25 years. West Glamorgan was asked to make gifts with a Welsh theme, to be presented to the delegates from 90 countries. A Clydach Guide patrol represented the county and was visited by delegates.

The county held its own international events to coincide with the World Conference. These included an international day at Swansea Museum, with many aspects of international

Four Ranger Guides from Neath who came second in a national festival of song in London. Kerrie Hopkins, Lorraine Horswill, Gillian Heycock and Karen Shelby represented Wales against competition from Guides across Britain.

Guides of the world

United and unique
Bound by the same Founder's rules
Are the black and the white
Guides, the Protestant, the Jew,
The sunbaked Australian,
The snow-bred Canadian,
The hard-working African,
The fortunate Briton.

All have a common theme,
Help others.

So do not despair you hungry
Sick and aged, for any
Moment now, someone will
Knock at your door,
Smiling faces will greet you,
Your worries are shared
For the Guides have come
Willing to serve.

Karen Wood

The chairman of West Glamorgan County Council, Councillor Martyn Thomas, and his wife with a group of Neath Brownies at Glynfelin, Longford, during celebrations to mark the Silver Jubilee of Queen Elizabeth in July 1977.

Guiding on display. In the evening there was a reception called A Taste of Wales. Guests included the Chief Commissioner for Wales, the Lord Mayor of Swansea and many public figures. The refreshments made and served by Rangers included Glamorgan sausages, cockle patties and mussel stew. The evening was a success and was brought to a close with some typical Welsh entertainment.

June 1974 brought with it the opening of the Penrice campsite hut. The money to construct this was raised by West Glamorgan Guides and Rangers and the buildings were opened free of debt. The first camp held there was an international one that attracted Rangers from Scandinavian countries and Canada.

A group of West Glamorgan Rangers and Guides performed an episode of The Legend of Arthur at Broneirion for delegates staying there after the World Conference.

This was also European Heritage Year and many Guides and Rangers took part in the Swansea Heritage Year scheme.

During this period many trainings were held throughout the county, along with a major one at Broneirion.

The county continued to provide trainers of a very high calibre, and these trainings were very important to unit Guiders in the planning of activities and the development of the Guides themselves.

117

Judith Shakeshaft of the 1st Aberafan Guides, receives her Patrol Camp Permit, 1978.

The Swansea Division was the largest in the county numerically and, as a result, a decision was made to split it into two. The two new divisions became Swansea Glantawe and Swansea Glanymor.

The year 1976 brought a sad time for everyone in Guiding with the death of the Chief Guide, Lady Olave Baden-Powell. Services of thanksgiving for her life were held all over the world. West Glamorgan held its service in Singleton Park on October 2, 1976. It was a simple but impressive event at which the Chief Guide's last message was relayed.

Guiding involved itself in many ways to celebrate the Queen's Silver Jubilee in 1977 and the Diamond Jubilee of the Rangers.

There were services of thanksgiving, a Jubilee camp at Broneirion, where Rangers from West Glamorgan won the Welsh quiz; a bed of roses was planted in Castle Gardens, Swansea, and the county was well represented at many prestigious Guiding events all over the country from Bala to Bath, from Wembley to York, and several meetings in London.

Many good deeds were being undertaken. Money was raised to help fund a new unit at Morriston Hospital for the treatment of Spina Bifida sufferers. As a result of this a Brownie from Morriston district was asked to cut the tape at its official opening.

Members of the 3rd Manselton Guides working for their Dairymaid badge, 1973.

The 30th Swansea Guides and Rangers prepare to set off for camp at Broneirion, 1977.

Nightingale Patrol of the 30th Swansea Guides with some of the items they made in their quest to win their Enterprise Pennant, March 8, 1974.

The last year of the decade, 1979, was designated by the United Nations as the International Year of the Child. This gave great scope to Guides and Guiders alike in the county for some excellent fund raising efforts.

As the year's designation suggests, its aim was the raising of money and the awareness of the situation of many children at home and abroad. This was achieved in many ways, such as by sponsored activities and gang shows.

Ranger Guides displayed information about the rights of the child in the window of the Dolphin Hotel in Swansea. All these activities resulted in the raising of a magnificent £4,900.

The county was very fortunate at this time to have a team of voluntary trainers, thus enabling trainings to take place as and when required locally. In addition four members of the Welsh advisory team were from the county.

The end of the 1970s saw Guiding in West Glamorgan going from strength to strength with excellent leaders at the helm. The originators of Guiding in the county, back in 1912, would have been proud to see this.

Members of the 3rd Port Talbot Brownie Pack who were divisional winners in the National Guide Festival of Song, 1972.

Recipes for celebration 12

When it comes to celebrations, members of Girlguiding West Glamorgan are up there with the best. As many will tell you without persuasion, there is no better way to salute an important event than to bake a cake. Round ones, square ones, rectangular-shaped ones, they have all made an appearance down the years. The centenary celebrations brought with them their fair share of tasty baking as units marked this milestone. Perhaps Guiding is one of the ingredients of a good cook!

Afan Valley Guiders Emily Jones and Rachael Thomas cutting a cake to celebrate the presentation of their Queen's Guide Awards, 2010.

Neath Trefoil Guild celebrated their 20th birthday in time-honoured fashion. Muriel Davies and Sarah Davies, the oldest and youngest members, had the privilege of cutting the cake.

Lady Olave Baden Powell officiates at a presentation ceremony during the Discoverer's Challenge Camp at Penrice May 29-31, 1964.

Much time, energy and effort went into the making of these wonderful creations so feast your eyes on some of those on the following pages.

Celebrations are also marked in lots of other ways. There have been many occasions when cakes have been accompanied by more formal tributes.

Some of those are featured here too and no doubt they will revive memories for many of those who were there at the time.

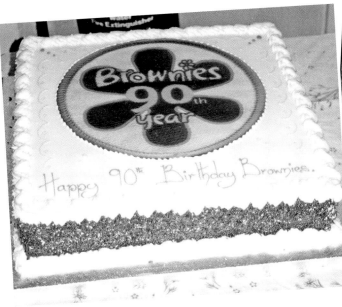

The cakes here are typical of the creativity that has been shown by many of West Glamorgan's capable cooks.

Faye Grinter,
1st Bishopston
Brownie Guider,
receives her Duke
of Edinburgh Gold
Award from
Phyllis Jamieson
at Parkmill on
February 20, 2011.

The 2nd Clydach
Guides had a tasty way
to celebrate the gaining
of Baden Powell
awards, 2007 – a giant
iced cake.

Miss E M Leonard receives a presentation in recognition of her remarkable 50 years in the Guide movement, 1966.

Dunvant Brownies at a tea party they held on HMS Achilles.

Betty Clement received a silver tea service and commemorative cake when she retired as Guide Guider at 2nd Sketty Guides, 1983. Her husband George Clement received a silver tankard.

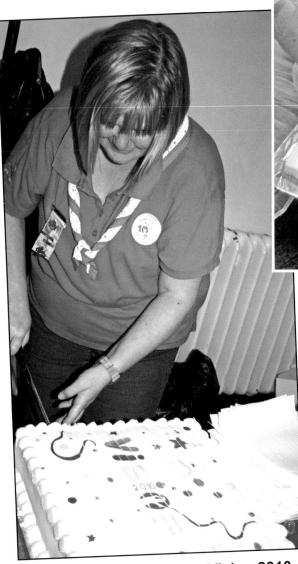

Celebrating the 21st anniversary
of Rainbows at Bryn Road Guide
Headquarters, Swansea, 2008.

I remember

. . . absolutely loving Guiding,
especially with the Guide age
group. I have enjoyed every job
I have done in the movement —
**Anne Faull, President Girlguiding
West Glamorgan, former County
Commissioner and Chief
Commissioner for Wales.**

Cutting the Afan Division Vision 2010
cake — with precision of course!

The message on the cake says it all!

Cimla Guide Sian Clwyd Roberts proudly shows her Baden-Powell award certificate, to her former 6th Neath Brownie Pack leaders Sue Scott, Brown Owl and Isobel Skinner, Tawny Owl, April, 1993.

This cake was baked to celebrate the 25th anniversary of Parkmill Guide Activity Centre.

Catherine Kwantes, County Commissioner, congratulates Maureen Blair who was retiring as District Commissioner for Mumbles, March 1963.

Colour Parties outside St Mary's Church, before a service to celebrate the 50th anniversary of the launch of Brownies, May 8, 1964.

A leaving party for Brown Owl Liz Daymond and Tawny Owl Ann Pike of Tonna Brownies, 1991.

Elizabeth Hartley, Deputy Chief Commissioner presents the Beaver Award to Catherine Kwantes, right, County Commissioner for West Glamorgan, at the Swansea Rover Ranger Conference, February 22, 1964.

Members of the 1st Mumbles Guides gather around Nerys Lloyd when she received her Young Leader certificate, January, 1990.

United we stand

13

From the earliest times of Girlguiding in West Glamorgan the movement has gone from strength to strength. Having started with a handful of units the county has grown into a force to be reckoned with. It has often been in the vanguard of change and development. Today, as the county bids farewell to the centenary celebrations of Girlguiding UK, and prepares for a year in which it will commemorate its own 100 year milestone, it can be proud that it has influenced the lives of thousands of young women. The pictures that follow feature most of today's 140 units.

1st Dunvant Rainbows — a really colourful group!

4th Killay Brownies

2nd Fforestfach Guides

2nd Gorseinon Brownies

2nd Morriston Brownies

1st Penclawdd Brownies

A member of
1st Cadoxton
Brownies
having a
great time.

1st Blaendulais
Rainbows, Brownies
and Guides not in their
traditional uniforms!

2nd Cimla Brownies

1st Birchgrove Rainbows

2nd Sketty Brownies

A 1st Cadoxton Brownie listens intently.

2nd Swansea (St James) Guides

18th Swansea Brownies

4th Killay Guides

1st Llansamlet Brownies

1st Bishopston Brownies

1st Briton Ferry Brownies

3rd Port Talbot Guides

3rd Clydach Brownies

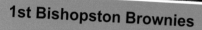

3rd Manselton Brownies

1st Manselton (St Michael's) Brownies

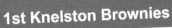

1st Knelston Brownies

1st Birchgrove Brownies

1st Llwchwr Rainbows

1st Baglan Rainbows

1st Gorseinon Brownies

5th Neath Guides

2nd Waunarlwydd Brownies

10th Swansea Guides

9th Morriston Brownies

25th Swansea Rainbows

3rd Port Talbot Rainbows

3rd Neath Brownies

1st Cwmavon Brownies

1st Gower Senior Section

1st Baglan Brownies

1st Brynhyfryd Rainbows

1st Grovesend Guides

2nd Port Talbot Guides

1st Three Crosses Brownies

3rd Aberavon Brownies

1st Loughor Brownies

3rd Pontardawe Guides

1st Three Crosses Guides

3rd Killay Brownies

1st Caewern Rainbows

3rd Neath Rainbows

4th Morriston Brownies

2nd Morriston Rainbows

1st Sketty Brownies

10th Swansea Brownies

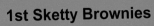

4th Sketty Brownies

1st Waunarlwydd Guides

1st Birchgrove Guides

3rd Loughor Brownies

1st Three Crosses Rainbows

2nd Sketty Guides

1st Clydach Rainbows

2nd Sketty Rainbows

1st Langland Brownies

4th Morriston Guides

**1st Cwmbwrla
Rainbows**

**1st Morriston
Brownies**

1st Danygraig Brownies

1st Trallwn Brownies

1st Waunarlwydd Brownies

13th Swansea Brownies

1st Fforestfach Brownies

25th Swansea Brownies

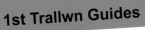
25th Swansea Guides

2nd Cimla Rainbows

1st Trallwn Guides

13th Swansea Rainbows

1st Caewern Brownies

5th Sketty (All Souls) Guides

5th Sketty (All Souls) Rainbows

30th Swansea Guides

140

1st Tonna Brownies

1st Rhos Brownies
at their 40th birthday
celebrations in 2011.

1st Rhos Rainbows

4th and 6th Morriston Guides

1st Manselton (St Michael's) Rainbows

2nd Clydach Guides

2nd Baglan Brownies

1st Neath Brownies

3rd Port Talbot (St Theodore's) Brownies

1st Townhill Brownies

1st Margam Rainbows
and Brownies

2nd Skewen Brownies

1st Gorseinon Brownies

1st Bishopston Guides

1st Killay Brownies

1st Mumbles Brownies

3rd Skewen Rainbows

1st Cwmbwrla Brownies

1st Hafod Brownies

Cila Rangers

1st Baglan Guides

Swansea West Rangers

1st Garden Village Brownies

Fun in the fresh air

14

Girlguiding in West Glamorgan, in keeping with the movement in general, has provided countless youngsters with the opportunity to experience life in the great outdoors through the adventures of camping. For many of these Guides, regular camping trips have offered the opportunity to learn survival skills, not only in the fullest sense, but also on a more personal level, where it has given them the chance to learn about, and demonstrate, how to look after themselves and others too.

There is always lots to do on Guide camp, as these girls of the 1st Bryncoch Company discovered in 1959.

Camp is where new friends are often made, and character-building outdoor pursuits experienced for the first time.

Camp sites have been located in a diverse range of places throughout the history of Girlguiding in West Glamorgan.

Units have gone to the countryside, to the beach, and even shared the experience on a grander scale with units from far and wide.

Many members will have fond memories of days spent at Penrice, Penmaen and Parkmill, Gower where down the years facilities have been created to enable camping and indoor holidays to be enjoyed.

A wonderfully graphic image of camping is provided by Viv Davies, a Guide in West Glamorgan for more than 20 years. Her recollections will strike a chord with many who followed in her footsteps on the path to adventure, and bring memories flooding back.

Morriston Rangers camping at Southerndown, 1927.

During the 1960s, camping and Pack Holidays continued to grow in popularity. They were always a favourite activity. Something many Guides and Brownies looked forward to with relish.

Viv tells how, in the 1950s, there wasn't a lot of money around, but despite this, children still had lots of fun. Even living in Swansea, a city struggling to rebuild after the war, there were lots of green spaces and old 'bomb sites' on which to play.

"At the age of 10 my friends and I decided to join the local Guide company and a new world opened out for us," said Viv.

"We loved our uniforms, with the brown leather belts having little metal clasps for whistles and penknives; we learned how to fold and iron our ties and brasso'd our badges so that we'd get points at 'Inspection' every week.

"I was in the White Heather Patrol – my best friend was in the Daffodils. We loved the running games, the nature hunts, and found that learning could be fun. It was so different from school. Even today I can find the North Star, know the history of how the Union Flag was put together, do simple First Aid and 'hospital corners' on my bedding. But my greatest love was the outdoor activities. The Saturday hikes – when we learned to light fires safely in the woods, cook a meal and leave the site as though no-one had ever been there. We each had a set of mini kits — a small tin of kindling, a tiny washing up kit, a sewing kit, even a tiny shoe cleaning kit.

"The annual camp was the highlight of my year and my only holiday. It cost about £2 and my Dad only earned £12 a week, but Mam scrimped and saved and off I went with everything squashed into my uncle's old Army rucksack. I was, as a little 10-year old, going to my first camp, and I could just about carry it to the bus – if I'd fallen over, I certainly couldn't have got up again! Oh! The excitement of getting our lovely green ridge tent up — the smell of the canvas and the challenge of keeping all our belongings off the ground for a whole week on little wooden gadgets, and not touching the tent sides when it rained in case you destroyed the tension.

"We were always too excited to sleep properly on the first night, and just as dawn was breaking, our patrol leader would let us get dressed. Shivering in our shorts and plimsolls we'd quietly leave the camp site and, to the sound of wood pigeons cooing, would go for a short walk. It was quite magical for us Townies.

"One year when we were camping on the edge of a plantation in Merthyr Mawr, a

Members of the 6th Swansea (Christ Church) Guide Company at camp in Penmaen, 1947.

147

A special badge created for visitors to two popular West Glamorgan camp sites.

Guides at a summer camp in Gower, early 1930s.

morning mist came out of the trees and surrounded us with the silence of nature. We went back to camp, collecting wood as we went, to get breakfast ready as the sun came up. We learned to be careful near the open cookhouse fire and how to cook 'Sunday Dinner' including a joint of meat for 30 people in big black and silver dixies. We sat in a horseshoe of groundsheets on the grass to eat, and sang lovely short graces. My favourite was Johnny Appleseed:

> *'The Lord is good to me,*
> *And so I thank the Lord,*
> *For giving me the things I need,*
> *The sun, the rain and the apple seed*
> *The Lord is good to me.'*

And we swatted at the wasps that wanted to share our food!

"On the Sundays we moaned each year about having to put on our full uniforms to go to the local church service. Looking back though, I've been in some beautiful country churches that I would never see again. The parishioners were always glad to see us overflowing out of the tiny pews into the aisles.

"The camp fires were fun, full of songs – and smoke, when the breeze went the wrong way. Very occasionally a Scout troop from a nearby camp would be invited to join us and there would be a few giggles mixed in with the songs and action skits. The camp fire would always be followed by prayers and Taps by the dying glow of the fire, then hot chocolate from a dixie which had been kept warm in a straw filled tea chest. Then it was off to our sleeping bags. Things have changed a lot since then. "The Guides are now even more environmentally minded and cook on stoves. Children today seem much more sophisticated, but the sense of fun and learning is still there. Of course, I loved it all so much! When it was time for me to leave, I carried on as a Ranger then as a Guide Guider . . . 20 years a Girl Guide. Thank you Olave and Robert Baden-Powell."

South Gower
District Rangers
at camp in
Penmaen, 1948.

Guides and Scouts pay attention at West Glamorgan's Scout/Guide camp in the summer of 1962.

Guides at camp in Penrice, Gower, 1937.

West Glamorgan Scouts and Guides at camp in Hatherop, Gloucestershire in the late 1960s. This was the first ever joint camp to be held outside the county. The Scouts and Guides were members of the 3rd Sandfields (Holy Trinity) units. The Scout and Guide leaders were Mr & Mrs Raymond Bray and Mr and Mrs Tony Morgan.

Helping to keep hungry mouths fed!

Nora Peacock who was a Guider for 29 years from 1951 to 1980. During this time she managed all the affairs and repairs of Providence, was Captain of the Bishopston Guide and Ranger Companies and regularly took her girls camping in Britain and abroad. She was a member of the Women's Royal Naval Service in the Second World War and lost a leg as a result of injuries received. Nora was awarded the MBE for her services to the Limbless Ex-Servicemen's Association.

Guides and leaders of the 1st Cimla Company camping at Saundersfoot, Pembrokeshire, 1956.

Having fun under canvas.

Swansea Sea Rangers at camp during a sailing weekend in Fishguard, 1950.

These members of 6th Swansea (Christ Church) Guides had a handy makeshift table for their meal at camp in Penmaen, 1947.

A group of Guides at the 1st Cimla Training Camp at Glynfelin, Longford, Neath, May 26, 1990.

Miss Ray Charles
is a qualified camper
Date Sept: 29th 1955
Norma J. Stride
Guider's Commissioner
Maureen R. S. Blair
Tester
Maureen R. S. Blair
C.A., I.HQ. or C.C.A.
or C.C.A. (Admin.)

Girls of the 30th Swansea Guide Company at camp in Mary Twill Lane, Newton, during the 1990s. The dog seems to be well trained too!

Brownies from the 2nd Morriston Pack having lunch during a sandcastle building event at Blackpill, Swansea during May 2010.

Kitchen duties at camp!

Songs and actions at an Afan camp fire evening, 2009.

Camping at Parkmill Activity Centre.

The 6th Swansea (Christ Church) Guides raising the flag at camp in Penmaen, 1947.

Bryncoch Guides at camp in Penrice, 1950s.

Exploits of the Eighties 15

Among highlights of the 1980s in West Glamorgan was the staging of an international camp at Margam Park, Port Talbot. Its clear aim was to spread a message of friendship and it proved a success. The decade also brought the official opening of the Parkmill Guide Centre, Gower, a major extension of facilities for a wide variety of activities. The county had now grown to become the third largest in Wales with an overall membership of 5,000, including Rainbows, Brownies Guides and Senior Section.

Ready for a cuppa ... a special tea party, organised by 5th Sketty Brownies, 1985.

Local camps and Pack Holidays were held, involving every age group. Many members also attended camps further afield, including international events.

In 1983 West Glamorgan hosted its own international camp at Margam Country Park, Port Talbot. The theme of this successful event was friendship, and there is no doubt that it generated many enduring links.

The camp proved a very worthwhile project for the county, but very hard work for the organisers. Around 850 Guides and Guiders camped at Margam, with visitors from 10 different countries. It was a wonderful experience for everyone.

Another successful event was held at the Morfa Stadium at Landore, Swansea – just across the River Tawe from the site of the present-day Liberty Stadium. It was a rally and fun run in aid of the new Olave Baden-Powell Centre for WAGGGS — the World Association of Girl Guides and Girl Scouts. A total of £4,722.53 was raised.

Rangers were now fulfilling a regular duty at Singleton and Morriston Hospitals every Sunday, wheeling patients down from the wards to services in the hospital chapels.

They were also enjoying the benefits of adventure weekends. Activities during these

A group of Neath District Guiders in their town centre divisional headquarters, 1985.

Guide leaders at a display organised by the county in the Quadrant shopping centre, Swansea, May 1983.

Guider Violet Vaughan of the 4th Port Talbot (Salvation Army) Guides at Margam Park international camp, 1983.

Guides who attended an international camp at Margam Park during their visit to County Hall in Swansea, where they were welcomed by West Glamorgan County Council Chairman, Tom Jones and his wife, 1983.

Guides taking part in the West Glamorgan Guide Carnival in Swansea, 1985.

Participants and spectators at Morfa Stadium, Landore, Swansea during a rally and fun run to raise money for the new Olave Baden-Powell Centre for WAGGGS — the World Association of Girl Guides and Girl Scouts.

Brownies enjoy a life on the ocean wave during a tea party aboard the Mumbles Inshore Lifeboat, 1985.

Afan Valley Division Commissioner Jean Gale presents Lisa Williams of the 3rd Port Talbot Company with her Queen's Guide badge in 1984. This was the last time this award was made in Port Talbot before the badge system changed.

included wind surfing, canoeing, sailing, hill walking, crafts and Celtic cooking. This was made possible by improvements in safety standards and more training for Guiders in outdoor pursuits. A growing number of Guiders were also obtaining camp licences.

It was about this time that the first County Archivist was appointed in order to gather as much information as possible about Guiding from its earliest times in West Glamorgan.

As well as the usual round of events, several unusual activities took place in this period – a Sport and Skate day in Pontardawe; a 50-mile walk along Offa's Dyke and the serving of strawberry teas.

Raising money for good causes is always high on the programme of all units, and among some of the fundraising efforts carried out during the 1980s was the Afan Valley Division's Good Turn during Christmas week which took the form of a trolley push, where Guides took trolleys back to the store from the cars of appreciative customers.

The Neath Division joined students of Neath College's catering department for a world sponsored pancake cook in aid of Cancer Research.

Meanwhile the Afan Valley districts of Baglan and Sandfields came up with another great idea, which must have proved worthwhile in many ways – a sleep-out in cardboard boxes

The 6th Neath Brownies mount a Guard of Honour at the wedding of their Snowy Owl Anita Bate to John Martell, July 25, 1987.

Civic hospitality for Danish visitors after an international camp at Margam 1983.

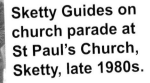

Sketty Guides on church parade at St Paul's Church, Sketty, late 1980s.

in aid of the homeless. A Guide with learning difficulties in the 2nd Clydach unit became a Young Leader, quite a challenge. The unit was congratulated on its foresight on integration and the Young Leader praised.

Young Leaders had now replaced the Cadet units of the 1960s and 70s. These girls were being trained to take over units when necessary. They were valued members of any unit, bridging the gap between Guiders and Guides and had hands-on experience of running a unit.

They could often be seen without their units at the poolside on Saturday mornings during Guide swimming sessions. There were about 75 Young Leaders working with Brownie and Guide units in West Glamorgan. The county was now awarding increasing numbers of Baden-Powell Badges. These were taking the

Nine members of the 1st Swansea (Fforestfach) Brownies, 1983.

These 1st Three Crosses Guides raised money for Comic Relief, 1989.

Brownies and Guides of the 2nd Sketty
Company are recorded for posterity, late 1980s.

The 6th Neath (Cimla) Brownies
pose for the camera, 1982.

Brownies gather at Cefn Saeson Comprehensive School, Cimla, Neath, for a Thinking Day celebration, 1988.

The 6th Neath Pack gather to celebrate 70 years of Brownies, November 1984.

Welsh cartoon character SuperTed and Port Talbot Mayoress Mrs Hilda Morgan attend a tea party during National Brownie Guide Tea Making Fortnight, with the 3rd Port Talbot (St Theodore's) Brownies, April, 1984.

place of Queen's Guide awards, which had passed into the Senior Section.

Trefoil Guilds were also opening up across the county. Guiders were now required to retire from uniform duties at 65, so many of them moved into the Trefoil Guild.

The year 1985 saw celebrations for the 75th anniversary of the founding of the Girl Guide movement. As usual West Glamorgan held many events to celebrate the occasion. There was a service on Thinking Day in the Brangwyn Hall in Swansea and an All-Wales eisteddfod - Dathliad or celebration - which

was held at Builth Wells. Competitors in this had successfully progressed through district, divisional and county competitions.

A Guide challenge was also set and 300 Guides qualified to camp at Penrice. For some it was their first experience of sleeping under canvas. Around 1,000 Brownies enjoyed a fun day at Neath, while Guide Week at the end of June saw the official opening of Parkmill as the county's new activity centre. During the week the 'Guiding Light' was brought to the county by the Chief Commissioner for Wales directly from Buckingham Palace.

West Glamorgan Guide Activity Centre, Parkmill, Gower.

WEST GLAMORGAN GUIDES

INVITE YOU TO THE

10 YEAR CELEBRATIONS OF

PARKMILL GUIDE ACTIVITY CENTRE

SATURDAY 24 SEPTEMBER, 1994 AT 7.00pm
PARKMILL GUIDE ACTIVITY CENTRE, PARKMILL

Tickets £2.00 to include light supper

Units held a seaside tide race during the 1980s to raise money for Parkmill Activity Centre. Those whose sand castle stood the longest won. It was great fun — with a serious cause.

Girls of the 1st Crynant Brownie Pack prepare for a balloon release.

Mumbles Coastguard Station was the venue for this special tea party event organised by 1st Manselton Brownies in 1985.

These 1st Sketty and Killay Brownies were cheering on fun run competitors.

Sunny day carnival fun, mid 1980s.

At the beginning of July there was a carnival with 30 marvellous floats. After much planning during the winter months the event was a great success. These events all helped to make the anniversary year one to remember.

With the last of the Meet the Gang productions taking place in 1981, the arts challenges became more localised, often district-based events. There were song and dance challenges, as well as drama, with trainings at Broneirion. Guides also participated in a number of operatic productions in Neath while Port Talbot District staged an Olde Tyme Music Hall.

The 75th anniversary of Brownies was also celebrated in many ways throughout the county. A fun day attended by 1,700 of them was held at Morfa Stadium, Swansea. Pool parties were now proving to be popular with Rangers, Guides and Brownies.

I remember
. . .My friends telling me about Brownies. It sounded great and I was very excited at joining. I'm a Sixer now and enjoy helping others —
Jennifer Smith, 1st Killay Brownies.

On the sporting front, Neath Division produced two champion teams, one winning the county swimming gala and one the county netball tournament.

The 1980s closed on a successful note. Parkmill was clear of debt after just four and a half years thanks to the hard work of all the units in the county in fund raising. It could now fulfil its great potential as a wonderful activity centre for future Brownies, Guides and Rangers.

By the end of the decade there was a new extension to the Guide family – Rainbows, a section catering for five to seven-year-olds. It filled an obvious need and immediately proved popular.

New wave Nineties

16

Looking back, most of those involved in Guiding would agree that the 1990s was a decade that brought a wave of change and challenge. It was one that saw the launch of new uniforms as well as a campaign to attract more people to wear them — at least at an organisational level. This was also a time when everyone in Guiding at both national and county level had to adapt to what was rapidly becoming the age of science and technology.

Walking for Wildlife, part of a World Wildlife Fund initiative, at Afan Argoed Country Park, 1995.

Since the inception of Guiding in 1910, the movement has always been prepared to move with the times and grasp new ideas for the benefit of the girls, and so science and technology advisers were appointed.

During the 1990s, more emphasis was placed on better co-operation between Scouting and Guiding. This had always been enjoyed in West Glamorgan, but it now became a priority nationally. A conference was held in York, the first ever for county commissioners of the Guide and Scout movements together.

Following up on this initiative, and with 1991 being the 75th birthday of Rangers, the Senior Section of the Guide movement, many joint activities were planned, such as Venture Scouts — the Senior Section of the Scout movement — attending county Ranger committees and vice versa, which led to jointly organised events.

The Rangers supported the Ventures in the United Nations peace campaign, Climb for the World. Many successful activities took place during this birthday year for Rangers.

At this time there were eight Ranger units active in the county. They were all involved in Celebration 91, taking part in both Fit for Fun and Strawberry Tea Camp. Rangers from Morriston and Mumbles also sang in the choir at the Thinking Day service at Westminster Abbey.

Many Rangers visited sites outside the county. One of these included a Ranger being invested on Skomer Island after seeing the Tall Ships Race, to camping at Broneirion, Waddow and Netherurd training centres, plus many more locations across the UK.

With the advent of the age of science and technology, Guides Cymru launched a Science Challenge for all sections, with many local units taking part.

The biggest challenge for all members of Guiding in Wales during the 1990s however, was to raise enough money to buy Broneirion, which had been used as the Welsh Training Centre since the 1940s. The amount of money needed was £500,000.

West Glamorgan has always been generous when it came to raising money for good causes. Now they had a chance to do something for themselves, and true to form the response to the appeal was remarkable. The county raised money in countless ways, such as May Day Millions, Tide Race, sponsored activities and many more.

County Commissioner Carol Clewett, with the chairman of West Glamorgan County Council, at a Baden-Powell presentation evening, June 28, 1994.

A Mount Pleasant Guide Company parents' evening around the camp fire at Penrice, 1990.

Some 1st Baglan and 2nd Port Talbot Guides experience what it is like to have a physical impairment during a disabled challenge event at Foxlease, 1993.

Windsurfing practice — on the grass!

In 1992 an international event, named Neptune Camp, was held at Penrice. Around 800 Guides came from all over Wales, with international Guides from Ireland, Poland, Hungary, Denmark and Czechoslovakia. The British Steel company sponsored the event and in return the Guides agreed to fill a skip with cans. Neptune was almost the last camp to be held at Penrice. The camp site held memories for so many Guides. It was the first in the county, leased to the movement by Lady Blythswood, a very strong supporter of Guiding until her death in 1958. It could be said that the camp site closed with a bang in true Guiding fashion.

Camping was then switched to the Penmaen site, also leased from Lady Blythswood, which the county was seeking to buy and upgrade.

West Glamorgan Guides were already lucky to have on their doorstep a beautiful activity centre at nearby Parkmill.

Friends and Young Friends of Parkmill worked very hard to raise money to continually improve the facilities at this centre, they continued to support it throughout the decade, providing a comfortable and safe environment for children, which was becoming more and more important as both the century and millennium drew to a close.

Following the success of the Neptune Camp there was a renewed interest in camping, with many Guide Leaders obtaining their camp qualifications with both long and short stay camps in the county, and others further afield at Foxlease. In 1993 a total of 19 camping qualifications were gained.

Neptune Camp, Gower, 1992.

Fresh air and fitness with fun thrown in too for these Brownies at Parkmill Guide Centre.

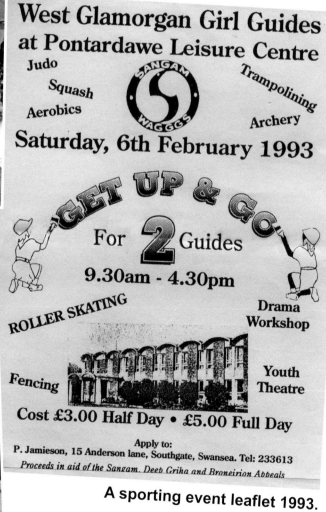

West Glamorgan Girl Guides at Pontardawe Leisure Centre

Judo
Squash
Aerobics

SANGAM WAGGGS

Trampolining
Archery

Saturday, 6th February 1993

GET UP & GO

For 2 Guides

9.30am - 4.30pm

ROLLER SKATING

Fencing

Drama Workshop

Youth Theatre

Cost £3.00 Half Day • £5.00 Full Day

Apply to:
P. Jamieson, 15 Anderson lane, Southgate, Swansea. Tel: 233613
Proceeds in aid of the Sangam, Deep Griha and Broneirion Appeals

A sporting event leaflet 1993.

Girls keep an eye on their
culinary efforts at Parkmill, 1991.

I remember
... Many happy times in Guiding, but will always cherish my involvement as director of the Neath Division production of Crystal Mania in 2001 where I met so many talented and enthusiastic youngsters.
— **Kirstie Roberts, former Cimla Brownie and Guide.**

Members of the Gower
Trefoil Guild, mid-1990s.

It was the county's turn to help at the Royal Welsh Show that year and 31 girls spent four days giving help where required with sheep, goats and cattle. This was followed up by Guides being on duty at the National Eisteddfod in Neath.

The 50th birthday of the Trefoil Guild was celebrated with many events. Guides across the county continued to be chosen to represent Wales abroad at international camps and gatherings.

In conjunction with the World Association of Girl Guides and Girl Scouts and the United Nations, Guides were asked to provide Peace Packs for refugees. Everyone took up the challenge and 700 packs were collected from West Glamorgan.

Brownies in the county took part in the Brownie quiz for the first time and it was a rewarding and instructive experience for all. The Guides had their chance by taking part in the Welsh Lamb challenge – cooking a meal on an open

Work underway
on refurbishment
of Bryn Road
Scout & Guide
headquarters,
June, 1990.

Members of the
2nd Port Talbot
Guides see the
sights during a
trip to London,
April 1997.

fire. It was quite a task but one that presented few problems for the patrols of this county.

Many girls were at this time achieving the Baden-Powell Trefoil Award, which was now the highest award in the Guide section.

West Glamorgan was afforded the honour of carrying the Welsh standard at the Thinking Day service in Westminster Abbey. A coach full of Guides and supporters went to London for the service, during which five of our Rangers sang in the choir.

Scout and Guide co-operation continued to flourish, with more Scouters attending such events as craft evenings and storytelling as part of the Year of Literature.

Forty-five Swedish Scouts came to Swansea for home hospitality after walking 100 miles in North Wales for their Explorer belt.

The activity centre in Parkmill had now been open for 10 years. Further plans involved the rebuilding of Ilston Lodge, which was opened on May 18, 1996, when 350 girls enjoyed a barbecue and campfire.

Many sections had the opportunity to take part in the Guides Cymru Environment Challenge, an important scheme to make them more aware of the threat to the environment.

Throughout the 1990s a lot of money was raised for county funds by a loyal band of workers at the Swansea Show on Spring Bank Holiday weekend. Programmes were sold and mountains of sandwiches were cut, with everyone standing for hours – usually in damp conditions – but it was all worthwhile at the end when the profits were counted up.

Many remember the laughs and the friendships of those occasions – such is the calibre of Guides, Guiders and supporters in the county of West Glamorgan.

A local newspaper printed several articles about everyday Guiding. This proved successful, and many new leaders and members were recruited as a result.

Leaders were attending trainings, many at Broneirion, which by now, Guides Cymru owned. Like any business it had to pay for itself, so the more it was used the better.

Smiles all round at a civic award ceremony, September, 1993.

Saying goodbye to old Penrice camp site . . .

. . . and hello to the new one at Penmaen.

171

During 1995-96 the county finally bought Penmaen campsite, while the Rainbow section celebrated 10 years as the youngest member of the Guide family, with activities centred around a Noah's Ark theme.

West Glamorgan joined the rest of Guides Cymru in 1997 to celebrate 50 years of Broneirion's status as the movement's training centre for Wales.

The Golden Jubilee celebrations saw the issuing of the Fifty Challenge Pack, which included something for everyone, from collecting 50 items to go in a time capsule to be opened in 50 years' time, to collecting 50 foreign coins for Childline.

Six members of the Senior Section went to Broneirion during the celebrations when Princess Margaret, President of the Guide Association, was visiting the Flower Festival. They sang and cooked Welsh cakes.

Providence Hall in Bishopston, a regular venue for Pack Holidays in the 1960s and 1970s, had a complete renovation and prepared to welcome a whole new generation of Brownies. The first Brown Owl of the pack that met there was present at the re-opening – she was 90 years of age.

A performance by the National Scout and Guide Orchestra was held in Swansea in 1997. County Guiders were saddened to realise that there were no instrumentalists from Wales – the Land of Song, after all – in the orchestra.

As a result the county executive generously set up an annual bursary scheme to help one player from the county who was accepted to join the orchestra. The first recipient was a member of the 4th Morriston Company.

The recruitment of leaders and girls became necessary during the latter part of the 1990s in order to guarantee a thriving movement to take Guiding into the 21st Century. The county rose to the challenge and a campaign was launched with a fashion show. Then the Rainbows and Brownies took up the challenge with 'Invite a Granny to Tea'. The campaign

Members of the 1st Rhos Rainbows at a My First Promise ceremony in June 1997 shortly after the re-opening of the group.

Six members of the 1st Neath Guides who received their Baden-Powell Trefoil awards at the same time, mid-1990s.

West Glamorgan Brownies and Guides in Swansea city centre during the Peace Packs campaign, 1995.

173

A group of 1st Neath Guides proudly display their newly won Baden-Powell awards. Among them, front left is internationally famous singer Katherine Jenkins who is also pictured alongside when she received a further award.

A group of 6th Mumbles Brownies take a rest on a walk to Pennard Castle, 1990s.

Pack Holiday took these members of the 1st Briton Ferry Brownies on a hike to Three Cliffs Bay, 1993.

Sketty Brownies and Rainbows with Esther Rantzen during the launch of Childline, 1991.

Members of the 1st Caereithin and 1st Cadle Brownies on Pack Holiday, 1999.

proved quite successful and several general offers of help were received as a result. By the end of the year 45 new Guiders had completed their training for a warrant, enabling new units to be opened. They were mostly in the Rainbow section, but others were also able to receive additional adult support.

The final year of the decade saw preparations for change to carry the Guide movement into the approaching new century and a new millennium, as well as plans for celebrations.

There were to be changes across the whole spectrum of Guiding and, as usual,

West Glamorgan was well prepared to embrace them. After all, they had been doing just that for more than 90 years since Guiding began in the county.

Many changes did take place during this period, and it may well be seen by future generations as the decade of science and technology.

As the 1990s came to a close, plans were well in hand for the Guide movement, at both national and county level, to celebrate the new millennium.

The Afan Valley standard which was dedicated on Thinking Day, February 22, 1999.

Representatives of West Glamorgan Senior Section at Westminster Abbey, London, February 20, 1999.

Into a new century 17

Girlguiding West Glamorgan marched into the first decade of the new millennium with gusto. At its helm, enthusiastically leading by example, was its commissioner Pamela Sutton. The dawn of the 21st Century saw the county join with Guides the world over in activities of celebration. Events included Thinking Day sessions, a gathering at the Brangwyn Hall, Swansea and a special mid-summer camp fire. Again, the county rose to the challenges that came with a new programme, new leadership qualification and a change of name — we were now all part of Girlguiding UK.

This patriotic bunch, mainly from West Glamorgan, raised a cheer for the Principality at the Wonderful One hundred Wales or WOW camp in Builth Wells, 2010.

A group of 1st Three Crosses Guides making willow baskets at the Wildfowl and Wetlands Centre, Penclacwydd, near Llanelli, 2000.

Renewal trainings were held at Broneirion at which the county was well represented, while at local level an evening was organised for Guiders to be brought up to date with the new qualification and 54 attended.

About two dozen established Guiders offered to help as mentors for new Guiders.

All branches of the movement celebrated the millennium in many ways with their units. They held daffodil tea parties, discos, raising money for HQs, wearing special T-shirts, outings, carnivals and much more.

An important part of the Guiding programme has always been community involvement and

Dark Horse Venture Challenge certificates were presented to members of West Glamorgan Trefoil Guilds in September 2002. From left are: June Shakeshaft, Margaret Seymour, Sylvia Thomas, West Glamorgan chairwoman Hilary Ferris, Wales chairwoman Margaret Routley, Mary Roberts, Shirley Williams and Janet Howells.

1st Cwmbwrla Rainbows on a visit to Cockett Police Station, 2004.

Afan Valley Division members waiting for the Queen to arrive at Margam Park, 2004.

the provision of support for good causes.
A challenge in the new programme was residential experience with their units, and 206 county Guides camped. Many took this up with visits to Parkmill, Our Chalet in Switzerland and other locations.

Trainings of all description were well attended, with the seven trainers in the county working hard on imaginative and interesting themes.

The West Glamorgan Guides Activity Centre at Parkmill continued to welcome girls of all ages to many and varied activities, while Trefoil Guilds remained active, supporting units in the county while enjoying a varied, and often

adventurous, programme themselves.
The county supported Book Aid International, a service project chosen by the Guide Association for the millennium year and 1,800 books were donated by West Glamorgan.

New Guide units were opened in Neath, while 30 Guides achieved the Baden-Powell Award. The Senior Section achieved two Queen's Guide awards, two gold and four bronze Duke of Edinburgh awards and 12 Chief Guide Challenge awards. There were 71 Young Leaders in the county.

West Glamorgan joined the rest of the Guide Association for a Day at the Dome in London.

This was a visit to the Millennium Dome. It was a great day and the gathering of so many blue and yellow uniforms was a spectacular sight.

Rainbows and Brownies were enjoying new and exciting experiences, such as visiting the Guide Heritage Centre, dancing with fans and feeding reindeer at Margam Park. Fund raising for good causes continued, with money donated to the Wales Air Ambulance.

Roadshows were held all over Wales to introduce the new Guide programme; 94 attended one at Pontardawe and 99 travelled to a similar event in Ystradgynlais.

The Senior Section continued to flourish, with two new Ranger units opening. Taster days were also held for 'Adventure Out'.

The Baden-Powell Trefoil was completed by 24 Guides – they were the last to do so before the syllabus changed.
There were also several Queen's Guide awards, Chief Guide Challenge awards and various leadership certificates during the year.

Camping was affected by the outbreak of foot and mouth disease, as restrictions were in place across much of the countryside, but alternative sites were found.

Every Rainbow loves a good story!

I remember

. . . having fun in Rainbows Go Wild. I like our Rainbow chat and all my friends in Rainbows
— Clara Tambini, 1st Margam Rainbows.

Members of the 2nd Port Talbot Guides tackle a challenge during Guide County Day at Margam Park Water World event, 2006.

Queens for a day!
Members of 1st
Cwmbrwla
Rainbows, 2007.

Good clean fun for
this 1st Three
Crosses Guide on a
muddy assault
course, 2002.

A 1st Cwmbrwla
Rainbow in the
stocks during a
visit to Neath
Museum at the
Gwyn Hall, 2004.

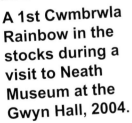

Members of the 5th
Sketty Guides at
Magic Camp,
Usk, 2002.

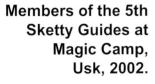

Guides from West Glamorgan were invited to international events in Sweden, the Ukraine, Denmark and Scotland. Units also camped in Switzerland.

Members of the 4th Killay Guides took part in the British Pedal Car Championships. Calling themselves The Pink Ladies, they raced over 24 hours and covered a distance of 202 miles. The Guides came 11th out of 16 but really enjoyed the challenge.

A modern version of the traditional gang show was produced by Rangers and Venture Scouts in Neath. It was an exciting spectacle of music and colour called Crystal Mania and more than 100 took part in what was universally saluted as a huge success. Gower division held a medieval fair day. It was all arranged via the internet, the girls learning many new skills suitable for the period.

The activity centre at Parkmill continued to be well used and well managed by an enthusiastic committee.

In 2002 the Guide Association was rebranded as Girlguiding UK. Welsh Guiding became Girlguiding Cymru, and West Glamorgan became Girlguiding West Glamorgan, with all five divisions in the county following suit. In 2002 the movement's President, Princess Margaret, died. The following year HRH Sophie, Countess of Wessex, daughter-in-law of the

Brownies Around the World was the theme of this special fun day at Parkmill, 2008.

Members of the 5th Neath Guides talking to the new West Glamorgan President, Anne Faull, at the celebration of 50 years of 5th Neath Guides, May 18, 2011.

As pretty as a picture – 2nd Cimla Rainbows all dressed up as princesses, 2010.

Queen, became the new President of Girlguiding UK. In this capacity she attended Guide events throughout the country and built up a sound relationship with the movement's younger members. There were royal visits to the county to coincide with the Queen's Golden Jubilee in 2002.

The highlight, from the girls' point of view, was a service held at St Mary's Church, Swansea attended by Princes Charles, William and Harry. Members of the movement were invited to the service and also to see the Queen at Margam Park.

Gnoll Country Park in Neath saw 147 Rainbows enjoy a day of activities in lovely sunshine. There was a footprint trail and duck feeding session.

The Brownies were introduced to their new programme, but continued to enjoy traditional activities as well. The Young Friends of Parkmill fun day with a Wizard of Oz theme was attended and enjoyed by 200 Brownies.

The Guides held adventure days with 85 Guides and 21 Leaders. All kinds of activities took place, from putting up a tent blindfold to various crafts. The Baden-Powell Challenge badge was achieved by 21 girls.

Some Senior Section units decided to hold monthly drop-in meetings, which fitted more

Young Leaders with members of the 2nd Morriston Brownies who made their Promise at a special Thinking Day service at Broneirion, February 2009.

Looking back

Choosing our activities,
Enjoying having fun,
New challenges we met,
The adventures now we've done.
Each and every one of us,
Neighbours far and near,
All making our own history,
Remembering THIS year.
Year of our Centenary –
memories we made
Will last with us forever,
And will never fade.

Memories of Centenary experiences from 1st Killay Brownies

183

Tonna Brownies ready to take part in the village's carnival as a dragon in 2001.

easily with their school commitments. However, they still worked enthusiastically towards bronze, silver and gold Duke of Edinburgh awards, attending Parkmill at weekends.

The section continued to attract new members, with 54 Young Leaders and 33 Rangers being registered across the county at the end of the first decade of the new millennium.

The Trefoil Guild was also busy. With the centenaries of Girlguiding UK and Girlguiding West Glamorgan approaching, they embarked on new and untried activities. Its members were awarded 14 Dark Horse certificates, including one gold.

Penmaen campsite continued to be upgraded, with many favourable comments from all who used it from within and without the county. A total of 215 camped in the county, and 100 camped outside it.

All divisions held their individual activities, ranging from raising money for the British Heart Foundation to holding themed international evenings for Thinking Day. The county continued to provide candidates to represent Wales at international camps abroad – these girls were, and still are, always of the highest calibre. The Rainbows had a new programme and continued to enjoy all

A brave Joyce Haydn Jones during a circus skills session at a Rainbows fun day.

County Commissioner Mary Knill at the annual general meeting, 2009.

Down to business – Girlguiding West Glamorgan's AGM, 2009.

aspects of Guiding appropriate to their age. A Circus Fun Day was attended by 81 Rainbows and 24 units took part in a challenge, ending with a Medieval Fun Day attended by 180 of them.

Brownies celebrated their 90th birthday in 2004 with parties and challenges and lots of fun, but they still had time to raise money for good causes and make interesting visits to places such as police stations and fire stations.

In 2006, the Senior Section celebrated their 90th birthday with many outdoor activities. Also that year, Mrs Liz Burnley became Chief Guide. Nearly 270 Guides camped with 174

Leaders and 80 in the Senior Section. Four Queen's Guide awards were achieved, and 16 gained their Chief Guide challenge. Five girls and four leaders represented West Glamorgan abroad. Support for members with disabilities

County Commissioner Mary Knill with some of her predecessors. From the left: Lesley Mathews, Carol Clewett, Anne Faull, Pamela Sutton, Mary Knill, and in front Joyce Haydn Jones.

remained an important part of the Guide programme, as had always been the case in West Glamorgan. As the decade drew to a close, it brought with it celebrations to mark 100 years of Girlguiding. This book not only mirrors that, but also a century of Girlguiding in West Glamorgan, a milestone in the 2012 calendar.

The fact that the movement, both nationally and locally, has survived a century of dedicated service through two world wars is the greatest tribute that can be paid. Those early Guides of 1910 may not instantly recognise their modern day counterparts, but nevertheless they all have one common bond – they are part of Baden-Powell's dream of a truly international organisation for young people, who have all made a Promise known to Rainbows, Brownies, Guides and Senior Section members everywhere. This really has been a century of Promises.

A flowerbed planted in Victoria Gardens, Neath, by the parks department of Neath Port Talbot Council to celebrate the Trefoil Guild's Diamond Jubilee in 2003.

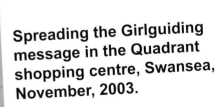

Spreading the Girlguiding message in the Quadrant shopping centre, Swansea, November, 2003.

Guilding the Trefoil

Among the most significant contributions to Girlguiding in West Glamorgan are those generated through the enduring enthusiasm of the county's Trefoil Guilds.
The main aim of those involved in the six current Guilds is to support their district units at the same time as providing friendship and activities for those involved. Membership offers opportunities to meet friends, develop interests, tackle new challenges, and help with district, division, county, national and international activities.

A walking group crosses the stepping stones at Three Cliffs Bay, wearing their UK Trefoil Guild scarves which were designed by Sheila Edwards, of Bishopston Guild. They were attending a county Trefoil event at Parkmill, October 2008.

Swansea

Swansea Diamond Jubilee greetings, 2003.

Pam Brown with the flower arrangement she made at the Vision event , Parkmill.

Guild members Rona Davies, Joan Tainsh and Anita Smith spending money at Ynysgain Guide Centre, near Criccieth, North Wales, March 2005.

Guild members at the county Vision 20:10 20/10 2010 event at Parkmill.

Swansea Guild members Elaine Kidwell and Ann Thomas on the bric-a-brac stall at a summer tea party at Parkmill, 2010.

Swansea members at the Eastern Bazaar table top sale at Glyn Clydach, November 2006.

Swansea Guild members at a county Fellowship Day lunch at the Dylan Thomas Centre, October 2009.

Mumbles

Although there are five Guiding divisions in West Glamorgan, the number of Trefoil Guilds in the county has increased to six – Swansea, Mumbles, Neath, Bishopston, Glantawe and Port Talbot – and the West Glamorgan Guild is now known as Swansea Trefoil Guild.

Swansea Trefoil Guild

When in 1982, Catherine Kwantes completed her term of office as Chief Commissioner for Wales, she embarked upon a project to establish the first Trefoil Guild in West Glamorgan. People were contacted, flyers were distributed, publicity obtained, and an inaugural meeting was arranged for March 29, 1982, at the Scout and Guide Headquarters in Bryn Road. As a result West Glamorgan Trefoil Guild was formed. Numbers were small at first, but grew gradually, thanks to the enthusiastic leadership of Mrs Kwantes and all those who succeeded her.

Today there is a membership of 40-plus, including three of the founder members, Bunny Adams, Heinke Griffiths and Jean Strawford. So it really is true that from little acorns…

Mumbles Trefoil Guild

The inaugural meeting of Mumbles Trefoil Guild was held on September 15, 1988, at 7pm in the United Reformed Church Hall.

Joyce Haydn Jones was the County Trefoil Guild Chairman and she gave the eight original members a short talk on the history of the movement and the aims of the Trefoil Guild.

Over the years the Mumbles Guild has fluctuated in membership and at present has 16 members. After 22 years they moved to All Saints Church Hall for their monthly meetings. Inevitably, they have lost many members over the past 22 years, and it was with sadness in November 2010 that they lost their past County Chairman, Guild Chairman and County President, Joyce Haydn Jones.

But they carry on as the Guide Law says: "A Guide smiles and sings under all difficulties."

Members of Mumbles Trefoil Guild during a tour of the Welsh Water sewage plant at Port Tennant, Swansea, 2010.

Mumbles Trefoil Guild members outside the Coastguard headquarters at Tut Head, 2010.

Members of Mumbles Guild enjoy afternoon tea outside a Langland Bay chalet.

The late Joyce Haydn Jones in Aberglasney Gardens, Carmarthenshire, 2008.

Members of Mumbles Trefoil Guild present a cheque to representatives of the Wales Air Ambulance service, 2003.

Neath

Neath Guild members enjoying a morning of Traditions of Guiding at Glynfelin, 2002.

Neath Trefoil Guild Easter bonnet competition, April 2006.

Neath Trefoil Guild

In 1986 Gwen Slee called a meeting at Carnegie Hall, Skewen, to start a Trefoil Guild in Neath. It was well attended and Mrs Kwantes, the chairman of West Glamorgan Trefoil Guild, spoke and gave a donation to start the Guild.

Gwen was the only person willing to become enrolled that afternoon. She became the leader and Mrs Ann George secretary. Meetings were mostly held in Gwen's house and although quite well attended, people were not totally committed to the Guild, and eventually even Gwen's enthusiasm began to waiver. In 1990 Pat Duncan, who had been a member of Fleet Trefoil Guild in Hampshire, contacted Gwen and Ann to form a Guild in Neath. Pat became chairman, Gwen treasurer and Ann secretary. Neath Trefoil Guild was registered on October 16, 1990. It celebrated its 20th birthday in October 2010 with a special lunch.

In 2010 the Guild took part in the Adventure 100 challenge. It produced a booklet on the history of the Guild. A centenary kneeler was also completed and dedicated at St Matthew's Church, Dyffryn, Bryncoch.

Neath Guild members making costumes for The Magic Clock gang show, 2002.

A Neath Guild afternoon tea at Neath Guide Hall where members and guests enjoyed an afternoon of Memories of Guiding.

Neath Guild visiting the recycling centre at Port Tennant as part of the Adventure 100 Challenge.

Bishopston

Selling Turkish Delight to Margaret Routley at the Eastern Bazaar, Glyn Clydach during West Glamorgan Fellowship Day celebrations, 2006.

Drumming in Glyn Clydach – West Glamorgan Fellowship Day celebration, 2006.

Bishopston Trefoil Guild

In 1997 Providence, the old chapel used by the Guides, Brownies and Rangers of Bishopston, was re-opened thanks to years of hard work by Sandra Pressdee, Guiders and the community. The old chapel was transformed from a damp, dreary, dilapidated stone shell into a welcoming, light and warm meeting place.

Many former Guiders saw the astonishing changes and it seemed a good idea to start a Trefoil Guild. The Bishopston Guild began in 1998 with just a small group of members.

In 2007 Providence was 200 years old. To celebrate the occasion, Sandra organised the making of a DVD about the history of Providence and Trefoil Guild members spent hours researching the archives.

One glorious summer evening, Trefoil members walked from the chapel in Newton, down through Caswell Valley and up to Providence, following in the steps of chapelgoers in the past.

The Guild members enjoy a varied programme, support units and have raised funds for several charities over the years.

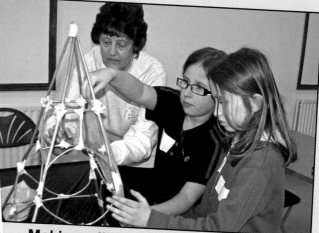

Making willow-framed lanterns for a film celebrating 200 years of Providence.

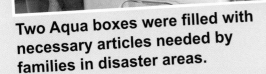

Two Aqua boxes were filled with necessary articles needed by families in disaster areas.

Trefoil Guild members took the Rainbows and Brownies on a flying carpet to try crafts from different regions.

Members from the county enjoyed a weekend break attending the 2009 Trefoil Guild Wales/Cymru AGM at RAF Valley, Anglesey.

Eileen Davies and June Bevan, doing the washing up at the Trefoil Guild Wales/Cymru AGM at Bryn Road, 2008.

Noreen Rees, Maggie Seymour and Joyce Haydn Jones at the UK Trefoil Guild AGM in Eastbourne, 2008.

West Glamorgan Trefoil Guilds 20:10 20/10 2010 Vision event centenary finale at Parkmill. Everyone enjoyed a good singsong.

SIGNALLING H..S BEEN CONDUCTED FOR LLOYD'S
AT BEACHY HEAD SINCE 1877.

THIS WATCH TOWER WAS LEASED BY THE
CORPORATION OF LLOYD'S
FROM
HIS GRACE THE DUKE OF DEVONSHIRE
IN DECEMBER 1882.

REBUILT BY LLOYDS IN 1896. PURCHASED BY LLOYD'S IN 1897,
AND FORMED A PART OF
LLOYD'S SIGNAL STATION AT BEACHY HEAD
UNTIL 1904,
WHEN SIGNALLING WORK FOR LLOYD'S WAS
TRANSFERRED TO THE ADJOINING NAVAL STATION
WHERE SINCE THEN IT HAS BEEN CONDUCTED FOR LLOYD'S.

**The Trefoil Guild Wales/Cymru
AGM in April 2008 was held at the
Bryn Road Scout and Guide HQ
in Swansea. Ann Thomas and
Joyce Haydn Jones are seen with
Councillor Susan Waller, left,
Lord Mayor of Swansea.**

**Joyce Haydn Jones, Fiona Lamb, Sheila
Edwards and Maggie Seymour brush up
on their semaphore skills at the UK Trefoil
Guild AGM in Eastbourne, 2008.**

**A gardening group at work during a
county event at Parkmill, October 2008.**

**Ray Charles, Diane Harry, Sylvia Thomas,
Winifred Morgan, Janet Howells, Neath
Guild, and Rhona Ray at the UK Trefoil
Guild AGM in Guildford, 1999.**

**County members enjoying an afternoon
of 'music for fun' at the Bryn Road
Scout and Guide HQ, Swansea, 2008.
This group celebrated its 10th
anniversary in February 2011.**

Glantawe

Glantawe Guild visiting Girlguiding HQ and the ICANDO exhibition in London as part of the Adventure 100 challenge Moving, 2010. The journey involved a shared day adventure by car, train and taxi, covering over 100 miles.

Glantawe Trefoil Guild

Glantawe Trefoil Guild started in 1998 with about 10 interested people. Miss Ray Charles came to the first meeting and supplied them with coffee, tea, sugar and milk. Their first meeting place was St David's Church Hall in Morriston, but later they moved to Aenon Baptist Church, Strawberry Place, Morriston.

They meet once a month and enjoy a varied programme. The last few years has seen them knitting furiously, producing, among other things, scarves, beanie hats, and glove puppet Teddy bears for the Samaritans Purse shoe boxes.

They have good relationships with the Guiders in the division and join in with division activities.

Glantawe Guild enjoying an evening in Mumbles and a visit to Verdi's.

Glantawe Guild knitted more than 100 hats and scarves for the Samaritans Purse Christmas shoe boxes as part of the Adventure 100 Challenge.

Daffodil making, 2009.

Glantawe Guild enjoying an evening stroll in Mumbles.

Port Talbot

Port Talbot Guild members at County Thinking Day Service, February 22, 2011.

Port Talbot Trefoil Guild

The present Port Talbot Guild was registered on September 9, 2008. It replaced one that closed in1990. Its members enjoy a varied programme of speakers, activities, and excursions. To begin the national centenary celebrations in September 2009, as part of the Change the World challenge, members took over the Save the Children shop in Cardiff for a day, providing clothing and bric-a-brac for the shop, learning the pricing system, pressing clothes and serving customers. Members joined others in West Glamorgan for a centenary exhibition at Swansea Civic Centre, and for the launch party at the LC, both in September 2009. The Guild was thrilled to join Afan Valley members for the Thinking Day event, One World, One Beat, and for the Centenary Closing Ceremony, Vision 20:10 20/10 2010.

At Christmas 2009, the Guild organised a Welcome to Christmas for Afan Valley Division Rainbows, Brownies, Guides and Senior Section members. This was enjoyed by everyone, with Guild members assisted by Guiders, running craft sessions, singing and drama. Port Talbot's special project for the centenary was a Centenary Recipe Book, published in time for Christmas 2009. It was a real hit, and so many were sold that a reprint was needed. Proceeds from the sale were divided between Guild funds and Trefoil's international fund, for assisting Guides to go camping abroad.

Members also made a scrapbook of their Guiding memories during centenary year.

Port Talbot Guild members ran the Save the Children shop in Cardiff for a day as their part in the Change the World project, September 9, 2009.

Port Talbot Guild members built towers to hold water as part of the Adventure 100 Challenge, April 13, 2010.

Members at a Queen's Guide presentation in Port Talbot Guide HQ on July 19, 2010.

Chairman of Trefoil Guild UK Margaret Routley, joins in as Port Talbot Guild members make Christmas cards November 11, 2008.

Swansea members at the Trefoil Guild Wales/Cymru AGM on Anglesey, April 2009.

West Glamorgan Trefoil Guilds 20:10 20/10 2010 Vision event centenary finale at Parkmill. Members renewed their Promise with Chief Guide Liz Burnley.

I remember

. . . Going to Belarus on a Gold project in 1997 to teach leaders about Guiding in the UK. I also worked at Pax Lodge in London. I had a lot of fun as a Brownie and a Guide, and I have made lasting friendships through the movement.

— Catherine Rubin, Trefoil Guild member.

Rainbows and Brownies on a flying carpet ride to try crafts from different regions, courtesy of Bishopston Trefoil Guild.

About our county 19

Girlguiding West Glamorgan has achieved much during its first 100 years. This ranges from the exploits of those individuals who founded the movement in the county, to grander accomplishments such as the staging of large events. Down the decades, many members have represented the county in different fields and travelled to far flung corners of the world. None of this would have been possible without the support of a committed band of organisers. A timeline of the county's history and look at some of those involved, past and present, provides a fitting close to this book.

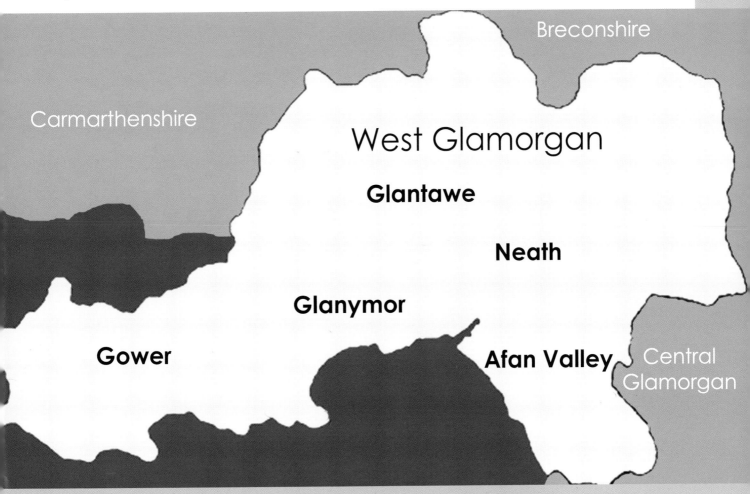

The Guiding county of West Glamorgan, its neighbours and its divisions.

Our county timeline

Girlguiding starts → 1909

1917 – Twelve Guide companies in Swansea

1912

Lady Olave Baden-Powell with Freda Gibbins, Neath Division Commissioner, at the opening of Neath HQ, 1964.

1959 – County President, Lady Blythswood, died. She was a Glamorgan Guiding pioneer

1960 – Golden Jubilee of Guiding

1964 – Neath Division becomes 1st to open its HQ

1970

1970 – Girlguiding in West Glamorgan has all time high of 4,926 members

1971 – Gang shows return to the county

1983 – County hosted international camp at Margam Country Park

1985 – around 1,700 brownies pack Morfa Stadium to celebrate their 75th anniversary

1912 – Girlguiding starts in West Glamorgan

1960

1961 – New County Standard dedicated

1980

1990

1992 – Neptune International Camp held at Penrice

1996 – county buys Penmaen campsite

1920 – Guides welcome King and Queen to Swansea

1920

1930

1936 – Second camp site opened at Penmaen

1921 – Penrice campsite opens

1937 – King and Queen visited the county in July

1940 – County Guides battle on during the Second World War

1940

1950

1958 – Swansea Air Rangers Flight starts

2010 – Centenary of Girlguiding UK

Past and present - back to 1910 was the theme of a camp at Penrice in 1985. These two Guiders dressed in original uniform for the event.

2012

2010

2012 – Centenary of Girlguiding in West Glamorgan

2000

2003 – Countess of Wessex became President of Girlguiding UK

2002 – Guide Association re-branded Girlguiding UK

and so to the future...

County administrators 2011

President
Anne Faull

Commissioner
Mary Knill

Secretary
Ann Evans

Treasurer
Nicola Lewis

Assistant Treasurer
Lynne John

Archivist
June Shakeshaft

PR Adviser
Diane Holohan

Outdoor Activities & Queen's Guide Adviser
Christine Thomas

Camp Adviser
Jenny Jones

Holiday Adviser
Pamela Sutton

Senior Section Adviser
Kay Dowdall

Guide Adviser
Victoria Ellis

Brownie Adviser
Rhian Matthews

Rainbow Advisers
Pamela Griffiths & Emily Jones

International Adviser
Stephanie Rutt

Duke of Edinburgh Award Adviser
Robert Thomas

Commissioner Support
Mary Levi

Membership Support
Sue Muxworthy

Leadership Qualification Adviser
Laura Williams

Guiding Development
Sue Scott & Jane Stubbs

Awards Facilitator
Pauline Morgan

Badge Secretary
Ann Morgan

County Trefoil Guild President
Hilary Ferris

County Trefoil Guild Chairman
Mary Roberts

Division Commissioners

Afan Valley
Suzanne Edwards

Glantawe
Jean Erasmus

Glanymor
Fiona Proudfoot

Gower
Joanne Allder

Neath
Janet Huxtable

District Commissioners

Afan Valley
No districts

Glantawe Division
Clydach & Morriston - Kelly Stephens
Swansea East - Pam Griffiths
Tawe - Helen Morris-Guy

Glanymor Division
Killay - Jan Ashford
Mumbles - Marilyn Hixson
Sketty - Carole Stockton
Swansea West - Alison Walley

Gower Division
Mid-Gower - Merle Howell
Rural Gower - Sally John
South Gower - Alison Hughes

Neath Division
Cimla - Sue Scott
Neath Rural - Amanda Burton
Dulais Valley - Carole Westall (Administrator)
Neath - Julie Edwards
Skewen - Jane Watkins
Vale of Neath & Glynneath - Katherine Jones

Past commissioners

Where records have allowed, here is a list of past commissioners:

County

1927 – 1944
Glamorganshire
Lady Blythswood, Penrice Castle, Reynoldston

1944 – 1957
West Glamorgan
Miss Freda Gibbins, Glynfelin, Neath

1957 – 1968
Mrs Catherine Kwantes

1968 – 1978
Mrs Jean Morgan

1978 – 1983
Mrs Joyce Haydn Jones

1983 – 1991
Mrs Anne Faull

1991 – 1997
Mrs Carol Clewett

1997 – 2002
Mrs Pamela Sutton

2002 – 2007
Mrs Lesley Mathews

2007 – 2012
Mrs Mary Knill

Division

Afan Valley
1927 – 1930
Mrs Andrew Fletcher, Margam Castle

1931 – 1937
Mrs E U David

1946
Mrs Broadway

194 8
Mrs Evans Bevan

1962
Mrs Tyler

1968
Mrs Surman Morgan

Gower
1927
The Hon Olive Campbell, Penrice Castle

1928 – 1929
Miss E Gold, Lansdown, Mumbles

1931 – 1942
The Hon Mrs Laurence Methuen

1946 – 1948
Mrs Picton Thomas

1950 – 1956
Mrs Morton

1959 – 1962
Mrs M H Morgan

1968
Mrs N Peacock

Neath
1927 – 1935
Mrs Theodore Gibbins, Glynfelin, Neath

1936 – 1942
Miss Freda Gibbins, Glynfelin, Neath

1946 – 1968
Miss Freda Gibbins, Glynfelin, Neath

Swansea
1927 – 1938
Mrs J T Davies, Kilgreen, Caswell Road, Mumbles

1939 – 1941
The Hon Mrs Laurence Methuen

1942 – 1946
Miss I G Hodgens, Gabalfa, Sketty, Swansea

1948 – 1957
Miss G M R Evans

1957 – 1968
Mrs Jean Morgan

1968
Mrs J Haydn Jones

Swansea Valley
1931 – 1942
Miss G Thomas

1946
Mrs G Bellingham
1948 – 1952
Mrs A J Jones

1965
Mrs Morris

1968
Mrs B Kiwenzler

Parkmill activity centre

The West Glamorgan Guides Activity Centre at Parkmill, Gower is one of the modern day jewels in the county's crown.

It is a hive of activity, a meeting place to be proud of, and caters for all sections of the movement, with an endless list of activities ranging from trainings to fun days and holidays.

The route to the activity centre that is known and loved by all who are involved with Girlguiding West Glamorgan began in 1983. That year Anne Faull became County Commissioner. It had been her long-time ambition that the county should have an indoor Guiding activity centre.

A number of sites had already been considered by members of the County Executive when West Glamorgan County Council announced that the former primary school building at Parkmill was no longer required as an outdoor pursuits centre for schools, and was to be sold. It was generally agreed that this was an ideal building and location for a county activity centre, for all sections to use for holidays. The sale of the property required the submission of sealed tenders, and much to everyone's delight, Girlguiding West Glamorgan's was accepted. It was at this point that the hard work really started. The county was now committed to serious fund-raising! This is where the

inspirational leadership of Anne Faull came in. Anne refused to be daunted by the scale of the work needed to transform the centre. As a result, with the efforts of all members in West Glamorgan and grants from various organisations, the centre was paid for in just four and a half years.

It was officially opened in 1985, with some of the loans still to be repaid, but by mid 1987 it was the county's! The former headmaster's house became a Ranger house, while the old school and Ilston Lodge were refurbished to accommodate larger groups.

From that point to the present day thousands of Rainbows, Brownies, Guides, Senior Section members, Guiders and Trefoil Guild members have visited the centre. These have not just been from West Glamorgan, or Wales, but from many parts of the UK and the world. They have all enjoyed its facilities, and the fun and friendship of residential events there. In addition they have been able to enjoy the wonderful surroundings and scenery offered by the beautiful Gower Peninsula.

Thanks to the efforts of the Warden, Phyllis Jamieson, the centre is used for Field Studies by school and college groups during weekdays in term time, when Guides and Brownies are not using it.

Inside the shop at Parkmill.

One of the meeting rooms at Parkmill. It was originally the old school hall.

A view of Ilston Lodge, summer, 2011.

West Glamorgan Guides Activity Centre and its attractive grounds, 2011.

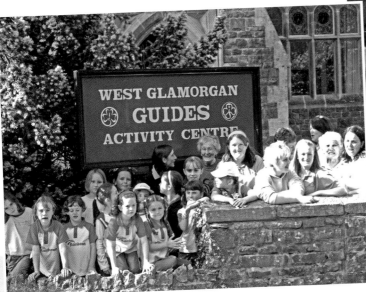

The sign outside the centre.

Some of the modern kitchen facilities at Parkmill, 2011.

The breathtaking view from Penmaen camp site, Gower.

Full list of units

The following list shows the names of those units, in both division and district order that existed at the time of the publication of this book in the autumn of 2011.

Most of these, Rainbows, Brownies, Guides and Rangers are featured pictorially in the chapter entitled United We Stand. During the history of Girlguiding West Glamorgan other units have been formed and in some cases existed for many years, but sadly are no longer operational.

Gower Division

Mid Gower District
1st Gorseinon Rainbows
3rd Gorseinon Rainbows
1st Llwchwr Rainbows
1st Pontlliw Rainbows
1st Garden Village Brownies
1st Gorseinon Brownies
2nd Gorseinon Brownies
1st Grovesend Brownies
1st Loughor Brownies
3rd Loughor (St David's) Brownies
2nd Pontlliw Brownies
1st Gorseinon Guides
1st Grovesend Guides
1st Gower Senior Section

Rural Gower District
1st Three Crosses Rainbows
1st Knelston Brownies
1st Penclawdd Brownies
1st Three Crosses Brownies
1st Three Crosses Guides

South Gower District
1st Bishopston Rainbows
1st Bishopston Brownies
1st Pennard Rainbows
1st Pennard Brownies
1st Bishopston Guides

Neath Division

Cimla District
1st Blaendulais Rainbows
1st Cimla Rainbows
2nd Cimla Rainbows
1st Blaendulais Brownies
1st Cimla Brownies
2nd Neath Brownies
6th Neath Brownies
7th Neath Brownies
1st Blaendulais Guides
1st Cimla Guides

Neath District
1st Briton Ferry Rainbows
1st Cadoxton Rainbows
3rd Neath Rainbows
1st Tonna Rainbows
1st Briton Ferry Brownies
1st Cadoxton Brownies
1st Neath Brownies
3rd Neath Brownies
1st Tonna Brownies
3rd Neath Guides
5th Neath Guides
Neath Division Rangers

Neath Rural District
1st Alltwen Rainbows
1st Caewern Rainbows
1st Rhos Rainbows
1st Alltwen Brownies
1st Bryncoch Brownies
1st Caewern Brownies
1st Rhos Brownies
1st Caewern Guides
3rd Pontardawe Guides

Skewen District
3rd Skewen Rainbows
2nd Skewen Brownies

Vale Of Neath District
1st Glynneath Rainbows
1st Glynneath Brownies
2nd Glynneath Brownies
2nd Glynneath Guides

204

in West Glamorgan

Glan Y Mor Division

Killay District
1st Dunvant Rainbows
1st Killay Rainbows
1st Killay Brownies
3rd Killay Brownies
4th Killay (St Hilary's) Brownies
4th Killay (St Hilary's) Guides
Cila Senior Section

Mumbles District
1st Mumbles Rainbows
1st Langland Brownies
1st Mumbles Brownies
2nd Mumbles Brownies
1st Mumbles Guides
2nd Mumbles Guides

Sketty District
2nd Sketty Rainbows
5th Sketty (All Souls) Rainbows
1st Sketty (Baptist) Brownies
2nd Sketty Brownies
4th Sketty (Wesley) Brownies
1st Townhill Brownies
1st Waunarlwydd Brownies
2nd Waunarlwydd Brownies
2nd Sketty Guides
5th Sketty (All Souls) Guides
30th Swansea Guides

Swansea West District
1st Gowerton (Temple URC) Rainbows
13th Swansea (St Barnabas) Rainbows
10th Swansea Brownies
13th Swansea (St Barnabas) Brownies
18th Swansea (Pantygwydr) Brownies
2nd Swansea (St James) Guides
10th Swansea Guides
1st Waunarlwydd Guides
Swansea West District Senior Section
Brynmill Senior Section

Glantawe Division

Clydach and Morriston District
1st Clydach Rainbows
2nd Morriston Rainbows
3rd Clydach (St Mary's) Brownies

1st Morriston (St David's) Brownies
2nd Morriston Brownies
4th Morriston Brownies
9th Morriston Brownies
2nd Clydach Guides
4th Morriston Guides
6th Morriston Guides

Swansea East District
1st Brynhyfryd Rainbows
1st Cwmbwrla (St Luke's) Rainbows
1st Manselton (St Michael's) Rainbows
25th Swansea (St Alban's) Rainbows
1st Brynhyfryd Brownies
1st Cwmbwrla (St Luke's) Brownies
2nd Fforestfach Brownies
2nd Hafod Brownies
1st Manselton (St Michael's) Brownies
3rd Manselton Brownies
25th Swansea (St Alban's) Brownies
2nd Fforestfach Guides
1st Manselton (St Michael's) Guides
25th Swansea (St Alban's) Guides

Tawe District
1st Birchgrove Rainbows
1st Birchgrove Brownies
1st Danygraig (Mt Calvary) Brownies
1st Llansamlet Brownies
1st Trallwn Brownies
1st Birchgrove Guides
1st Trallwn Guides

Afan Valley Division
1st Baglan Rainbows
1st Margam (St David's) Rainbows
3rd Port Talbot (St Theodore's) Rainbows
3rd Aberafan Brownies
1st Baglan (St Catharine's) Brownies
2nd Baglan Brownies
1st Cwmavon Brownies
1st Margam (St David's) Brownies
3rd Port Talbot (St Theodore's) Brownies
1st Baglan Guides
2nd Port Talbot Guides
3rd Port Talbot (St Theodore's) Guides
Afan Valley Senior Section

Promises we make

as Rainbows

I promise that I will do my best to love
my God and to be kind and helpful.

Brownies

I promise that I will do my best:
To love my God,
To serve the Queen and my country,
To help other people, and
To keep the Brownie Guide Law.

Guides

I promise that I will do my best:
To love my God,
To serve the Queen and my country,
To help other people, and
To keep the Guide Law.

and Senior Section

I promise that I will do my best:
To love my God,
To serve the Queen and my country,
To help other people and
To keep the Guide Law,
And to be of service in the community.

Laws we keep

Brownies

• A Brownie Guide thinks of others before herself and does a good turn every day.

Guides

• A Guide is honest, reliable and can be trusted.

• A Guide is helpful and uses her time and abilities wisely.

• A Guide faces challenge and learns from her experiences.

• A Guide is a good friend and a sister to all Guides.

• A Guide is polite and considerate.

• A Guide respects all living things and takes care of the world around her.

Appreciation

Girlguiding West Glamorgan would like to thank all those who in however small a way have contributed to the work involved in making this book possible.

Among these people must be counted the late Rhona Ray, who produced the original manuscript from which this book has grown, as well as current Girlguiding West Glamorgan Archivist June Shakeshaft, who valiantly picked up where Rhona left off.

We appreciate the fact that the UK Chief Guide, Gill Slocombe, and Guides Cymru Chief Commissioner, Felicity Ladbrooke have written such kind words at the start of this book.

Our gratitude is also extended to: West Glamorgan County Archivist Kim Collis; Archives staff David Morris and Anne-Marie Gay; David Roberts, of Bryngold Books for turning what was once only a dream into a reality of which we can all be proud; the South Wales Evening Post for giving Rhona Ray permission to use some of the older images in the book along with some, more recent images; West Glamorgan Trefoil Guild Chairman, Mary Roberts, for her efforts in the compilation of the Trefoil Guild chapter; Judith Oakley, of Oakley Natural Images, for taking modern day photographs at Parkmill; the members of the committee involved in the commissioning and production of the book who shared in the headaches and heartaches. They are Mary Knill, Ann Morgan, Ann Chilcott, June Shakeshaft, Victoria Ellis, Rhian Matthews, Pam Griffiths, Diane Holohan and Kay Dowdall.

Finally, and by no means least, our thanks go to all those who from the very start contributed to make all aspects of Girlguiding West Glamorgan possible, and those who are ensuring that we can move into the next 100 years with as much zest and passion as those first pioneering Girl Guides!

Hats off to the past, sleeves up for the future!
– Lady Olave Baden-Powell, World Chief Guide